CLASSIC SERMONS
ON
JUDAS ISCARIOT

KREGEL CLASSIC SERMONS Series

KREGEL CLASSIC SERMONS SERIES

CLASSIC SERMONS ON JUDAS ISCARIOT

Compiled by
Warren W. Wiersbe

kregel
PUBLICATIONS

Grand Rapids, MI 49501

Classic Sermons on Judas Iscariot,
compiled by Warren W. Wiersbe.

Copyright © 1995 by Kregel Publications. All rights reserved. No part of this book may be reproduced, stored in
a retrieval system, or transmitted in any form or by any
means—electronic, mechanical, photocopy, recording, or
otherwise—without written permission of the publisher,
except for brief quotations in printed reviews.

Published by Kregel Publications, a division of Kregel,
Inc., P.O. Box 2607, Grand Rapids, MI 49501. Kregel Publications provides trusted, biblical publications for Christian
growth and service. Your comments and suggestions are
valued.

Cover photo: Copyright © 1995 Kregel, Inc.
Cover and book design: Alan G. Hartman

Library of Congress Cataloging-in-Publication Data

Classic sermons on Judas Iscariot / compiled by
Warren W. Wiersbe.
     p.   cm.— (Kregel classic sermons series)
    Includes index.
    1. Judas Iscariot—Sermons. 2. Sermons, American.
3. Sermons, English. I. Wiersbe, Warren W. II. Series:
Kregel classic sermons series.
BS2460.J8C57   1995   232.96'1—dc20   95-7814
                                                   CIP
ISBN 0-8254-4060-2 (pbk.)

1 2 3 4 5 Printing / Year 99 98 97 96 95

Printed in the United States of America

CONTENTS

LIST OF SCRIPTURE TEXTS

PREFACE

THE *KREGEL CLASSIC SERMONS SERIES* is an attempt to assemble and publish meaningful sermons from master preachers about significant themes.

These are *sermons*, not essays or chapters taken from books about themes. Not all of these sermons could be called "great," but all of them are *meaningful*. They apply the truths of the Bible to the needs of the human heart, which is something that all effective preaching must do.

While some are better known than others, all of the preachers whose sermons I have selected had important ministries and were highly respected in their day. The fact that a sermon is included in this volume does not mean that either the compiler or the publisher agrees with or endorses everything that the man did, preached, or wrote. The sermon is here because it has a valued contribution to make.

These are sermons about *significant* themes. The pulpit is no place to play with trivia. The preacher has thirty minutes in which to help mend broken hearts, change defeated lives, and save lost souls; and he can never accomplish this demanding ministry by distributing homiletical tidbits. In these difficult days we do not need "clever" pulpiteers who discuss the times; we need dedicated ambassadors who will preach the eternities.

The reading of these sermons can enrich your spiritual life. The studying of them can enrich your skills as an interpreter and expounder of God's truth. However God uses these sermons in your life and ministry, my prayer is that His Church around the world will be encouraged and strengthened by them.

WARREN W. WIERSBE

And Judas Iscariot

John Wilbur Chapman (1859–1918) was ordained a Presbyterian minister and served churches in Ohio, Indiana, New York, and Pennsylvania. He was a pastor who did the work of an evangelist and was greatly blessed of God. He ministered with D. L. Moody and was associated for ten years with Charles Alexander, the well-known Christian musician. They made a world tour that resulted in thousands coming to Christ. Chapman was the first director of the Winona Lake (Indiana) Bible Conference, and also assisted the conferences at Montreat, North Carolina, and Stony Brook, Long Island, New York.

This sermon is taken from his book, *And Judas Iscariot, Together with Other Evangelistic Addresses,* published in 1906 by Jennings and Graham, Cincinnati.

John Wilbur Chapman

1

AND JUDAS ISCARIOT

And Judas Iscariot (Mark 3:19).

THERE IS SOMETHING ABOUT the name of this miserable man which commands our attention at once. There is a sort of fascination about his wickedness, and when we read his story it is difficult to give it up until we have come to its awful end. It is rather significant, it would seem to me, that his name should come last in the list of the apostles, and the text, "And Judas Iscariot," would suggest to me not only that his name was last, but that it was there for some special reason, as I am sure we shall find out that it was. It is also significant that the first name mentioned in the list of the apostles in this third chapter of Mark was Simon, who was surnamed Peter.

The first mentioned apostle denied Jesus with an oath, the one last referred to sold Him for thirty pieces of silver and has gone into eternity with the awful sin of murder charged against him. The difference between the two is this: their sins were almost equally great, but the first repented and the grace of God had its perfect work in him and he was the object of Christ's forgiveness; the second was filled with remorse without repentance and grace was rejected. The first became one of the mightiest preachers in the world's history; the second fills us with horror whenever we read the story of his awful crime.

Different names affect us differently. One could not well think of John without being impressed with the power of love; nor could one consider Paul without being impressed first of all with his zeal and then with his learning. Certainly one could not study Peter without saying that his strongest characteristic was his enthusiasm. It is helpful to know that the Spirit of God working with one who was a giant intellectually and with one who was profane and ignorant accomplished practically the same results, making them both, Paul and Peter, mighty men whose ministries have made the world richer and better in every way. But to think of Judas is always to shudder.

There is a kindred text in this same Gospel of Mark, but the emotions it stirs are entirely different. The second text is, "And Peter." The crucifixion is over, the Savior is in the tomb, poor Peter, a brokenhearted man, is wandering through the streets of the city of the King. He is at last driven to the company of the disciples, when suddenly there rushes in upon them the woman who had been at the tomb, and she exclaims, "He is risen, has gone over into Galilee and wants his disciples to meet him." This was the angel's message to her. All the disciples must have hurried to the door that they might hasten to see their risen Lord—all save Peter. And then came the pathetic and thrilling text, for the woman gave the message as Jesus gave it to the angels and they to her, "Go tell his disciples—*and Peter*."

But this text, "And Judas Iscariot," brings to our recollection the story of a man who lost his opportunity to be good and great; the picture of one who was heartless in his betrayal, for within sight of the Garden of Gethsemane he saluted Jesus with a hypocritical kiss; the recollection of one in whose ears today in eternity there must be heard the clinking sound of the thirty pieces of silver; and the account of one who died a horrible death, all because sin had its way with him and the grace of God was rejected.

The scene connected with his calling is significant. Mark tells us in the third chapter of his Gospel that when Jesus saw the man with the withered hand and healed him, he went out by the seaside and then upon the mountain, and there called His apostles round about Him, gave them their commission, and sent them forth to do His bidding.

In Matthew 9:36–38, we are told that when He saw the multitudes He was moved with compassion, and He commissioned the twelve and sent them forth that they might serve as shepherds to the people who appeared to be shepherdless. "Then saith he unto his disciples, The harvest truly is plenteous, but the laborers are few; pray ye therefore the Lord of the harvest, that he will send forth laborers into his harvest." And then He sent the Twelve forth. As a matter of fact, the Scriptures concerning Judas are not so very full, but there is a good outline, and if one but takes the points presented and allows his imagination to work in the least, there is a story which is thrilling in its awfulness.

The four Evangelists tell us of his call, and these are practically identical in their statement except concerning his names. Matthew and Mark call him the Betrayer; Luke speaks of him as a Traitor, while John calls him a Devil. The next thing we learn concerning him is his rebuke of the woman who came to render her service to Jesus as a proof of her affection. In John 12:4–6, we read, "Then saith one of his disciples, Judas Iscariot, Simon's son, which should betray him, Why was not this ointment sold for three hundred pence, and given to the poor? This he said, not that he cared for the poor, but because he was a thief, and had the bag, and bare what was put therein."

Next we hear of him bargaining with the enemies of Jesus for his betrayal. The account is very full in Matthew 26:14–16. "Then one of the twelve called Judas Iscariot, went unto the chief priests, and said unto them, What will ye give me, and I will deliver him unto you? And they covenanted with him for thirty pieces of silver. And from that time he sought opportunity to betray him."

Then we are told of his delivering Jesus into the hands of his enemies in Matthew 26:47–49: "And while he yet spake, lo, Judas, one of the twelve, came, and with him a great multitude, with swords and staves, from the chief priests and elders of the people. Now he that betrayed him gave them a sign, saying, Whomsoever I shall kiss, that same is he: hold him fast. And forthwith he came to Jesus, and said, Hail, Master; and kissed him." And then finally comes his dreadful end, the account of his remorse in Matthew 27:3–4. "Then Judas, which had betrayed him, when he saw that he was condemned, repented himself, and brought again the thirty pieces of silver to the chief priests and elders, saying, I have sinned in that I have betrayed the innocent blood. And they said, What is that to us? see thou to that." And the statement of his suicide in Matthew 27:5, "And he cast down the pieces of silver in the temple, and departed, and went and hanged himself."

A Natural Question: Why Was He Chosen?

The natural question that comes to every student of the life of Judas must be, "Why was he chosen?" but as Joseph Parker has said, "We may well ask why were we chosen ourselves, knowing our hearts as we do and appreciating our weakness as we must." It has been said that if we study the apostles we will find them representatives of all kinds of human nature, which would go to show that if we but yield ourselves to God, whatever we may be naturally, He can use us for His glory. It was here that Judas failed. I have heard it said that Jesus did not know Judas' real character and that He was surprised when Judas turned out to be the disciple that He was; but let us have none of this spirit in the consideration of Jesus Christ. Let no man in these days limit Jesus' knowledge, for He is omniscient and knows all things. Let us not forget what he said Himself concerning Judas in John 13:18, "I speak not of you all; I know whom I have chosen; but that the Scripture may be fulfilled, He that eateth bread with me hath lifted up his heel against me." Again, in John 6:70, "Jesus answered them, Have not I chosen you twelve, and one of you is a devil?" and finally, in 6:64, "But there are some of you that believe not. For Jesus knew from the beginning who they were that believed not, and who should betray him."

There were others who might have been chosen in his stead. The apostles found two when in their haste they determined to fill the vacancy made by his betrayal. Acts 1:23–26, "And they appointed two, Joseph called Barsabas, who was surnamed Justus, and Matthias. And they prayed, and said, Thou, Lord, which knowest the hearts of all men, shew whether of these two thou hast chosen, that he may take part of this ministry and apostleship, from which Judas by transgression fell, that he might go to his own place. And they gave forth their lots; and the lot fell upon Matthias, and he was numbered with the eleven apostles."

It seems to me that there can be no reason for his having been called of Christ except that he was to serve as a great warning to those of us who have lived since his day. There are many such warnings in the Scriptures.

Jonah was one. God said to him, "Go to Nineveh," and yet, with the spirit of rebellion, he attempted to sail to Tarshish and we know his miserable failure. Let it never be forgotten that if Nineveh is God's choice for you, you can make no other port in safety. The sea will be against you, the wind against you. It is hard indeed to struggle against God.

Jacob was a warning. Deceiving his own father, his sons in turn deceived him. May we never forget the Scripture which declares, "Whatsoever a man soweth that shall he also reap."

Esau was a warning. Coming in from the hunt one day, weary with his exertions, he detects the savory smell of the mess of pottage, and his crafty brother says, "I will give you this for your birthright," which was his right to be a priest in his household; a moment more and the birthright is gone; and in the New Testament we are told he sought it with tears and could find no place of repentance. But many a man has sold his right to be the priest of his household for less than a mess of pottage, and in a real sense it is true that things done cannot be undone.

Saul was a warning. He was commanded to put to death Agag and the flock, and he kept the best of all the flock and then lied to God's messenger when he said that the work had been done as he was commanded. He had no sooner said it than, behold, there was heard the bleating of the sheep and the lowing of the oxen. "Be sure your sin will find you out."

The New Testament has many warnings like these in the Old, but Judas surpasses them all. There is something about him that makes us shudder.

It is said that in Oberammergau, where the Passion

Play is presented, the man taking the character of Judas is always avoided afterward. He may have been ever so reputable a citizen, but he has been at least in action a Judas, and that is enough.

I was once a pastor at Schuylerville, New York, where on the Burgoyne surrender ground stands a celebrated monument. It is beautiful to look upon. On one side of it in a niche is General Schuyler, and on the other side, if I remember correctly, General Gates; on the third, in the same sort of a niche, another distinguished general is to be seen, but on the fourth the niche is vacant. When I asked the reason I was told that "It is the niche which might have been filled by Benedict Arnold had he not been a traitor."

The story of Judas is like this. He might have been all that God could have approved of; he is throughout eternity a murderer, and all because grace was rejected. Numerous lessons may be drawn from such a story. Certain things might be said concerning hypocrisy, for he was in the truest sense a hypocrite. Reference could be made to the fact that sin is small in its beginnings, sure in its progress, terrific in its ending, for at the beginning he was doubtless but an average man in sin, possibly not so different from the others; but he rejected the influence of Christ. Or, again, from such a character a thrilling story could be told of the end of transgressors, for hard as may be the way the end baffles description. Judas certainly tells us this.

Judas May Be a Warning but There Are Four Things to Be Said Concerning Him

However much of a warning Judas may be to people of the world, I am fully persuaded that there are four things which may be said concerning him.

First: He gives us a lesson as Christians. There were many names given him. In Matthew 10:4 and in Mark 3:19, we read that he was a betrayer; in Luke 6:16 he was called a traitor; in John 6:70 he is spoken of as a devil, but in John 12:6 he is mentioned as a thief. To me, however, one of the best names that could be applied to him is that which Paul feared might be given to him when he said, "Lest when I have preached to others I myself should be [literally] disapproved" (1 Cor. 9:27). It is indeed a solemn thought, that if we are not right with God He will set us aside, for He cannot use us. I have in mind a minister, who once thrilled great numbers of people with his message. Under the power of his preaching hundreds of people came to Christ. There was possibly no one in the church with a brighter future. Today he is set aside, for God cannot use him. I have in mind a Sunday school superintendent, who used to be on every platform speaking for Christ, and then yielded to undue political influence of the worst sort, lost his vision of Christ and his power in speaking, and today is set aside. But of all the illustrations, I know of nothing which so stirs me as the story of Judas. He might have been true and faithful and he might have been with Christ today in glory; instead, he is in hell, a self-confessed murderer, with the clinking of the thirty pieces of silver to condemn him, and his awful conscience constantly to accuse him. It is indeed enough to make our faces pale to realize that, whatever we may be today in the service of God, we can be set aside in less than a week, and God will cease to use us if we have anything of the spirit of Judas.

Second: I learn also from Judas that environment is not enough for the unregenerate. It is folly to state that a poor lost sinner simply by changing his environment may have his nature changed. As John G. Woolley has said, "it is like a man with a stubborn horse saying, 'I will paint the outside of the barn a nice mild color to influence the horse within.'"

The well on my place in the country some years ago had in it poisoned water. It was an attractive well with a house built around about it; and the neighbors came to me to say that I must under no circumstances drink from it. What if I had said, "I will decorate the well house that I may change the water?" It would have been as nonsensical as to say, "I will change the environment of a man who is wicked by nature, and thereby make him good." Judas had lived close to Jesus, he had been with Him on the mountain, walked with Him by the sea, was frequently with Him, I am sure, in Gethsemane, for we read in John 18:2, "And Judas also, which betrayed him, knew the place: for Jesus ofttimes resorted thither with his disciples." He was also with him at the Supper. But after all this uplifting, heavenly influence of the Son of God he sold Him for silver and betrayed Him with a kiss. Nothing can answer for the sinner but regeneration. His case is hopeless without that.

Third: Hypocrisy is an awful thing. The text in Galatians is for all such. "Be not deceived; God is not mocked." Those words in Matthew in connection with the sermon on the Mount are for such, when men in the great day shall say, "Have we not prophesied in thy name? and in thy name have cast out Devils? and in thy name done many wonderful works?" Jesus will say, "I never knew you."

If we read the commission in Matthew 10:5–12 inclusive, we shall understand that these apostles were sent forth to do a mighty work, and evidently they did it. Judas had that commission, and he may have fulfilled it in a sense, but he is lost today because he was a hypocrite. The disciples may not have known his true nature. In John 13:21–29 we read, "When Jesus had thus said, he was troubled in spirit, and testified and said, Verily, verily, I say unto you, that one of you shall betray me. Then the disciples looked one on another, doubting of whom he spake. Now there was leaning on Jesus' bosom one of his disciples, whom Jesus loved. Simon Peter therefore beckoned to him, that he should ask who it should be of whom he spake. He then lying on Jesus' breast saith unto him, Lord, who is it? Jesus answered, He it is to whom I shall give a sop when I have dipped it. And when he had dipped the sop, he gave it to Judas Iscariot, the son of Simon. And after the sop Satan entered into him. Then said Jesus unto him, That thou doest, do quickly. Now no man at the table knew for what intent he spake this unto him. For some of them thought, because Judas had the bag, that Jesus had said unto him, Buy those things that we have need of against the feast;

or that he should give something to the poor." Which would seem to impress this thought upon us. Oh, may I say that it is a great sin to be untrue?

The only time that Jesus is severe is not when sinners seek Him out, nor when the woman taken in adultery is driven to Him by those who would stone her with stones, nor with the thief on the Cross, but when He faces hypocrites; He can have no tenderness for them.

Fourth: I learn from Judas that sin is of slow progress. There may have been first just a natural ambition. He thought that the kingdom of Jesus was to be a great temporal affair, and he desired to be a part of it. How many men today have wrecked their homes and all but lost their souls, because of unholy ambitions! It may be an ambition for your family as well as for yourself. Doubtless Jacob had such when he stopped at Shechem. The result of his tarrying was his heartbreaking experience with the worse than murder of his daughter. There are souls today in the lost world who were wrecked upon the rock of ambition.

Fifth: He was dishonest. It is a short journey from unholy ambition to dishonesty. The spirit of God Himself calls him a thief. But,

Sixth: Let it be known that while sin is of slow progress, it is exceedingly sure. In Luke 22:3–6 we read that Satan entered into Judas. It seems to me as if up to that time he had rather hovered about him, tempting him with his insinuations, possibly causing him to slip and fall in occasional sins, but finally he has control and then betrayal, denial and murder are the results.

I looked the other day into the face of a man who said to me, "Do you know me?" and I told him I did not, and he said, "I used to be a Christian worker and influenced thousands to come to Christ. In an unguarded moment I determined to leave my ministry and to become rich. My haste for riches was but a snare. I found myself becoming unscrupulous in my business life and now I am wrecked, certainly for time—oh," said he, "can it be for eternity? I am separated from my wife and my children, whom I shall never see again." And rising in an agony he cried out as I have rarely heard a man cry, "God have mercy upon me! God have mercy upon me!"

Three Things Yet to Say Concerning Judas

There are but three things that I would like to say concerning Judas as I come to the end of my message.

The first is that he was heartless in the extreme. It was just after a touching scene recorded in Matthew 26:7–13, "There came unto him a woman having an alabaster box of very precious ointment, and poured it on his head, as he sat at meat. But when his disciples saw it, they had indignation, saying, To what purpose is this waste? For this ointment might have been sold for much, and given to the poor. When Jesus understood it, He said unto them, Why trouble ye the woman? for she hath wrought a good work upon me. For ye have the poor always with you; but me ye have not always. For in that she hath poured this ointment on my body, she did it for my burial. Verily I say unto you, Wheresoever this gospel shall be preached in the whole world, there shall also this, that this woman hath done, be told for a memorial of her."

It was after this that Judas went to the enemies of Jesus and offered to sell him, and as if that were not enough, it was just after he had left Gethsemane, in Matthew 26:45–49, that he betrayed him with his kiss. "Then cometh he to his disciples and saith unto them, Sleep on now, and take your rest; behold, the hour is at hand, and the Son of man is betrayed into the hands of sinners. Rise, let us be going: behold, he is at hand that doth betray me. And while he yet spake, lo, Judas, one of the twelve, came, and with him a great multitude, with swords and staves, from the chief priests and elders of the people. Now he that betrayed him gave them a sign, saying, whomsoever I shall kiss, that same is he: hold him fast. And forthwith he came to Jesus, and said, Hail, Master; and kissed him." The blood drops had just been rolling down the cheeks of the Master, for He sweat, as it were, great drops of blood; and I can quite understand how upon the very lips of Judas the condemning blood may have left its mark. But do not condemn him; he is scarcely more heartless than the man who today rejects Him after all His gracious ministry, His sacrificial death, and His mediatorial work of nineteen hundred years.

Second: His death was awful. Acts 1:18, "Now this man purchased a field with the reward of iniquity; and falling headlong, he burst asunder in the midst, and all his bowels gushed out." I can imagine him going out to the place where he is to end it all, remembering as he walked how Jesus had looked at him, recalling, doubtless, some of His spoken messages, and certainly remembering how once He had been with him in all his unfaithful ministry. All this must have swept before him like a great panorama, and with the vision of his betrayed Master still before him he swings himself out into eternity; and then as if to make the end more terrible the rope broke and his body burst and his very bowels gushed forth. Oh, if it be true that the *way* of the transgressor is hard, in the name of God what shall we say of the end?

Third: I would like to imagine another picture. What if instead of going out to the scene of his disgraceful death he had waited until after Jesus had risen? What if he had tarried behind some one of those great trees near the city along the way which He should walk, or, possibly on the Emmaus way? What if he had hidden behind some great rock and simply waited? While it is true that he must have trembled as he waited, what if after it all he had simply thrown himself on the mercy of Jesus and had said to him, "Master, I have from the first been untrue; for thirty pieces of silver I sold thee and with these lips I betrayed thee with a kiss; but Jesus, thou Son of David, have mercy upon me"? There would have been written in the New Testament Scriptures the most beautiful story that the inspired book contains. Nothing could have been so wonderful as the spirit of Him who is able to save to the uttermost, and who never turned away from any seeking sinner, and He would, I am sure, have taken Judas in His very arms; He, too, might have given him a kiss, not of betrayal, but of the sign of His complete forgiveness, and Judas might have shone today in the city of God as shines Joseph of Arimathaea, Paul the apostle, Peter the preacher.

The saddest story I know is the story of Judas, for it is the account of a man who resisted the grace of God and must regret it through eternity.

NOTES

The Traitor Who Sold Him

William E. Sangster (1900–1960) was the "John Wesley of his generation" as he devoted his life to evangelism and the promotion of practical sanctification. He pastored in England and Wales, and his preaching ability attracted the attention of the Methodist leaders. He ministered during World War II at Westminster Central Hall, London, where he pastored the church, managed an air-raid shelter in the basement, and studied for his Ph.D. at the London University. He served as president of the Methodist Conference (1950) and director of the denomination's home missions and evangelism ministry. He published several books on preaching, sanctification, and evangelism, as well as volumes of sermons.

This message comes from *They Met at Calvary*, published in 1956 by Abingdon Press, Nashville.

William E. Sangster

2

THE TRAITOR WHO SOLD HIM

THERE IS A TERRIBLE SOUND in the word "traitor." A traitor is the very opposite of a loyalist; and the more we love loyalty, the more we loathe a traitor. In this hard world, men expect to be shot at by their enemies, but no one but a cynic expects to be shot at by his friends. And our Lord was no cynic. In all the heaped-up pain of His passion, few things hurt Him more than to be betrayed by one of His own men.

It Has Been Found Hard to Understand the Mind of Judas Iscariot

To our Lord's pain in his betrayal, we must add a good deal of perplexity in subsequent ages among Christians too. They have found it hard, through the years, really to understand the mind of Judas Iscariot.

It may be that his part in this cosmic tragedy was only a minor one. If mighty forces were bent upon the arrest and death of Jesus Christ, and if Jesus Christ had no intention to resist their evil will, the part of the man who said: "I know where he is; I can lead your soldiers there," is not a major one. Sooner or later, we may assume, His enemies would have got Him. If Judas had not acted as a guide, some other informer outside the apostolic band would have been found.

But the perplexities do not center chiefly in that.

It perplexes us that anyone who had known Christ with intimacy, who had lived with Him, talked with Him, walked with Him, eaten with Him, and watched Him at work, could do so foul a thing.

It perplexes us, in the second place, that anyone could do so foul a deed for so small a bribe. Thirty pieces of silver! The sum, of course, was not fixed at random. Thirty pieces of silver, as laid down in the Old Testament, was the price of a slave. In the currency of today (it has been calculated), twelve dollars. Good God! You wouldn't sell a dog you loved for twelve dollars! The reward seems so dreadfully out of proportion to the deed.

It perplexes us, in the third place, because there are passages in Scripture which leave us wondering if Judas was a free agent in this ghastly crime, passages which seem almost to suggest that he was born to do this dire deed and could not escape his destiny.

These are the uncertainties, and not these alone, which have made it so hard for Christians through fifty-seven generations to understand the mind and motives of Judas Iscariot.

Some Have Tried to Set Judas in a Kindlier Light Than Scripture Does

In an effort to evade these difficulties, some Bible students have been making suggestions concerning Judas which set him in a kindlier light than the Scriptures do, which aim almost at whitewashing him, which set out to prove that he was not quite the man he appears to be. These attempts began in early times, but they were popularized in England by De Quincey a century ago.

I think I have read them all. I hope I have read them with a reasonably open mind. The chief of these theories run like this:

1. Judas is said by some to have been an honest patriot who had come to the conclusion that Jesus was a danger to the nation; and he betrayed Him, therefore, out of pure love for Israel. What he did, these apologists say, may seem foul to us, but it was the outcome of an honestly mistaken judgment.

2. He is said, by others, to have been a loyal but impatient disciple, completely confident in our Lord's ability to extricate himself from any situation. Had he not seen a hungry multitude fed with a few loaves? Had he not seen the sick made well and the dead raised up? How could he help but have the supremest confidence in his Lord's capacity to deal with any folk who wanted to arrest Him

against His will. And the whole purpose of the betrayal, they argue, was to precipitate the events Judas desired, by putting Jesus in the kind of peril which would compel Him to display His sovereign power.

3. Still others hold a similar theory, though they express it in a slightly different way. Judas Iscariot, they argue, being in close touch with the people, knew that after Palm Sunday the people were on the very point of insurrection. Unhappily, from his point of view, our Lord seemed at that very season to become a procrastinator. He did not act as Judas thought He should. Instead of striding on from the popular acclaim of Palm Sunday to an open announcement of Himself as the King of Israel, He slipped into a kind of retirement, and spent a whole day at Bethany when He should have been among the people, stirring them up. Judas, therefore, brought the soldiers to Gethsemane, these students argue, so that Jesus might be forced to end His procrastination and step out as the King of Glory; and though Judas was wrong there, he was wrong in judgment and not wrong in heart.

4. Finally, there are those who argue that Judas was wavering in his conviction of the messiahship of our Lord. At moments he was sure; at other moments he was quite unsure. He remembered the wonders Jesus had done, but then he remembered also what the Pharisees and Sadducees were saying about him, and the question that shaped itself in his mind was this: "Is He the Messiah or not?"

How could that question be resolved? Judas came to believe that it could be resolved in only one way. Let Him be put to a test. Let Him be arrested on a capital charge, and then, if He was the Messiah, all His mighty power would flash out, and He would be seen as such. If He was not the Messiah, then He was a terrible impostor and deserved what He got.

Those, I think, are the major efforts that have been made—with a good deal of variation—to explain the perplexities concerning Judas Iscariot which have troubled Bible students for centuries. I find them, frankly, more ingenious than convincing. I believe that many of them are the fruit of a desire in preachers to say something new rather than to say something true. The impressive objection to them all is this: each one of them, on major points, runs counter to the Scriptures.

We know nothing about Judas Iscariot outside the Gospels. If we are to understand and interpret his character, we must sit close to the evidence as we have it. We may find things difficult to explain and inferences unpleasant to draw, but to escape from those difficulties by scorning the evidence is not serious exposition. It is doing violence to the Word of God.

Let us look, then, at some of the facts concerning Judas Iscariot which are laid down in Holy Scripture. John says: "He was a thief." Luke says: "Satan entered into him." Jesus says: "It would have been better for him if he had never been born." Pleasing as it is that Christian preaching should be eager to say the kindest thing it can about the world's most famous traitor, we must, nonetheless, keep to the evidence, and one part of the evidence, alas, is in these sayings. Whatever conclusions we draw must be in harmony with the Scriptures. What was the truth about Judas Iscariot? Basing ourselves on the Bible, what picture do we have at the last?

Judas Was the Only Judean

Notice, in the first place, that Judas Iscariot was the only Judean in the apostolic band. All the others were Galileans. Observe that. It is not unimportant. Of the twelve men Jesus chose "that they might be with him," eleven of them came from the north of the country, and one from the south. The southerner was Judas Iscariot. He spoke with a different accent. It is possible that he felt a little bit on his own from the start.

Notice also that he was a man of some commercial acumen. So it seems; for our Lord appointed him their accountant, the keeper of the bag. Their company, as it moved from place to place, was a company of thirteen. (That is probably the origin of the superstition concerning the number thirteen. Thirteen sat down to the Last Supper, and one of them was a traitor. Superstitious people have dreaded the number thirteen ever since.)

When a company of that size moves from place to place, it is better for one person to handle expenses; it saves trouble for the company and for the folk they are dealing with. Judas Iscariot was that man. He had business ability and our Lord made use of it.

It is impossible for us to believe that our Lord chose Judas *in order that he might betray Him.* That does not harmonize with the character of Jesus. If you believe that our Lord's incarnation involved some lack of knowledge (and we remember that there were things He Himself confessed He did not know, and that He expressed surprise on a number of occasions), then it will present no difficulty to your mind that He chose Judas Iscariot with the same affection as He chose the others, and trusted him in a position of responsibility.

If, on the other hand, you believe that our Lord carried long foreknowledge of all these events—and that John 6:64 means that Jesus knew the destiny of Judas from the beginning of His ministry—you will still remember that foreknowledge is not the same thing as foreordination. I know that the sun will rise tomorrow morning, but my knowing it does not make it rise. And it was at least possible for our Lord to know that Judas Iscariot would betray Him, without the knowledge compelling Judas to act as he did. He still acted for reasons of his own and with as much freedom as we human beings ever enjoy.

The painful truth appears to be that Judas Iscariot was a covetous man, that avarice was his sin. We are told that he had been pilfering in the bag some time before there was any talk of his betraying our Lord; the accountant had turned embezzler. He could even hide his greed under the cloak of piety. When Mary of Bethany brought that pound of spikenard and anointed the feet of Jesus, Judas Iscariot was the only one who could not see the inwardness and love of it all. He said, as though he had been shocked by the extravagance: "Why was not this ointment sold for three hundred pence, and given to the poor?"

How pious it sounds!

But John tells us that he did not really care for the

poor. If the price of the ointment had gone into the bag
which he was keeping, there would have been a little
more for him to pilfer. Our Lord, with the shadow of the
cross upon Him, said: "Let her alone: against the day of
my burying hath she kept this. For the poor always ye
have with you; but me ye have not always."

After Palm Sunday, and when Jesus began plainly to
disappoint the hopes of his disciples of an earthly kingdom, Judas Iscariot, as I sadly believe, came to the conclusion that there was nothing in this Jesus business—no
money, anyhow. It was all a farce. He had thought, when
he left his village and joined with the rest of them, that
this was going to lead on to fame and fortune. The only
outcome of it that he could see now was no fortune and a
good deal of infamy. However, he could make a bit out of
it. Not much! Thirty pieces of silver. . . . So he went to the
high priest and made the deal.

Perhaps it did not work out just as he had expected.
Maybe he only promised at first to take them to the Garden and thought that the soldiers would do the rest; but
as they drew near, they saw a cluster of people together,
and the soldiers did not know which one of the group to
take. Judas had to help them again—even more perhaps
than he wished. He said: "The one whom I kiss is he." He
went forward therefore—was ever the symbol of love so
utterly prostituted?—and kissed him into their arms.

"So they took him away."

We all know the terrible remorse that broke over Judas
Iscariot later. Did it come to him immediately? When he
saw our Lord suffer arrest meekly and permit them to
march Him off, did the great horror leap up at once in his
soul?

It seems that he followed his Master and may have
waited outside the hall of the Sanhedrin during the farce
of a trial. As the chief priests were leaving the Hall of
Hewn Stone, Judas stopped them, holding the money still
in his hands. "I have sinned," he cried, "in that I have
betrayed the innocent blood." But they passed on, spurning him. He had played his unimportant part and to them
he mattered no more. He ran after them, and before the

door of the sanctuary completely closed, he hurled the coins at their backs. Then, with a rope in his hands, he disappeared into the dark.

Things We Should Learn from the Story of Judas Iscariot

Does the story of Judas Iscariot speak in any way to our own need?

We learn from it, I think, that it is possible to live near to Christ and then to fall away. We learn that it is possible to be in His company, and be regarded as one of His intimates, and then to be guilty of the foulest betrayal. If any man, in some place of security, asserts in self-confidence that "nothing could happen to me here," that man has added, by his overconfidence, to the danger we mortals are always in.

I never go to Aber Falls in North Wales without feeling the pathos of something that occurred there years ago. A brilliant young lawyer, of whom I knew, was climbing the mountain near Aber Falls with a friend. His friend noticed the green slime on the rocks as they climbed and called out: "Do be careful," to which the young Mr. Payne replied: "Oh it's as safe as anything. *I couldn't* fall here." They were the last words he uttered. I know the spot at the bottom of the Falls where his mangled body was picked up.

We may infer, in the second place, that it is possible to be in the church of God and yet not be a disciple in heart. Was Judas ever a disciple in heart? Who can answer that question? Did he respond, in the first place, out of a deep and sincere devotion to our Lord and fall away in His company, or did he begin with low motives and never capitulate to Him in heart?

No one can answer that question concerning Judas Iscariot, but it is not to be doubted that people can be in the church today without any serious commitment to Christ in their heart. Indeed, their lack of loyalty can be concealed almost from themselves. Until some severe test comes, they are like everybody else. But a trial comes and they are revealed. Some folk have professed allegiance to our Lord and His church, but when a chance of earthly advancement has presented itself, they have turned their back on him and the things for which He stands, and taken the chance. Every Christian should periodically question his own soul: "Am I really in this because of devotion to my Lord? Would I stand if a crucial test came?"

There is a third thing to bear in mind. With some natures there is nothing so holy that money cannot besmirch it. Watch money. It is so enormously useful and so terribly dangerous. The Bible does not say that money is the root of evil but it does say that the *love* of money is the root of evil.

Finally, we may learn, I think, from the sad story of Judas, how wrong it is ever to limit our Lord's forgiveness. After the betrayal, Judas took his own life. He forgot his betrayed Master's message of forgiveness. Perhaps he was not listening when Jesus said that the love of God was so mighty that it would always meet penitence with pardon. Perhaps he was wondering whether there was enough in the bag to take a little more!

But knowing what you know of the forgiveness of God, do you think that if Judas had gone, not to hang himself, but to the cross, and flung himself before our dying Lord and said, "Lord Jesus, forgive me"—if he had done that, do you think that Christ who prayed for His murderers as they nailed Him to the wood, and who said to the dying thief, "Today shalt thou be with me in paradise," that that same Savior would have refused forgiveness to the man who had kissed Him into their arms?

I cannot believe it. It was the crowning error of Judas' miserable life.

Do not add that sin to any others you may have committed. Do not be like the man with whom I wrestled recently to a late hour, who, having reviewed the enormities of his past, denied that God would forgive him, and went out, as Judas went out into the night, with the mark of Cain on him and without faith that God would ever wipe it away.

Put no limit to the grace of God!

NOTES

The False Friend

Clovis Gillham Chappell (1882–1972) was one of American Methodism's best-known and most effective preachers. He pastored churches in Washington, DC; Dallas and Houston, Texas; Memphis, Tennessee; and Birmingham, Alabama; and his pulpit ministry drew great crowds. He was especially known for his biographical sermons that made biblical figures live and speak to our modern day. He published about thirty volumes of sermons.

This message was taken from *Faces about the Cross*, reprinted in 1971 by Baker Book House.

Clovis Gillham Chappell

3

THE FALSE FRIEND

Judas Iscariot, who became a traitor (Luke 6:16).

OF ALL THE FACES that we see about the Cross, there is none other quite so tragic as that of Judas. Not only is his a tragic face, but it is one that is vastly baffling and perplexing. This is evidenced by the fact that those who look into that face do not always come away with the same impression. A few see in Judas a blundering and mistaken hero, but the vast majority see only an inhuman scoundrel. These latter shut their eyes to all the good that was in him. They remember only one single act of his pathetic pilgrimage, his betrayal of his Lord. This, it seems to me, is not quite fair. Therefore, I am going to ask you to look at him again, forgetting for the present, so far as possible, the one black blot upon his life.

Three Simple Assertions About Judas

About this man Judas I think we may safely make three simple assertions.

1. Judas was not a monster, but a man. He was just as human as ourselves. This sounds trite, I know, but such is not in reality the case. We who are decent and respectable are constantly prone to look upon those who go vastly wrong as being entirely different from ourselves. They are made of the slime and ooze of things, while we are made of far finer material. It is hard for us to realize our kinship with one who betrayed his Lord. For instance, G. Campbell Morgan is easily one of the great expository preachers of our day. Many have both heard and read him to their enlightenment and edification. Listen to what he has to say about this false friend of Jesus. "I do not believe that Judas was a man in the ordinary sense of the word. I believe that he was a devil

33

incarnate, created in history for the nefarious work that was hell's work."

There have no doubt been many through the centuries who have felt this way about Judas. But, of course, we cannot agree. Such an explanation raises far more questions than it settles. If Judas were created an incarnate devil, if he were sent into the world to be a traitor to Jesus, then he is not to blame for being what he was, and doing what he did. He is no more to blame than the vessel that has been spoiled by the potter is to blame.

> They sneer at me for leaning all awry:
> What! did the Hand then of the Potter shake?

Who under these circumstances is to blame? The only answer is God. But this view we cannot accept. God never created any man either a monster or a devil. Traitors and scoundrels are not born, but made. We must, therefore, believe that Judas was a man.

2. Not only do we assume that Judas was thoroughly human, but we assume further that he was not always a traitor. Luke tells us that he became a traitor. He was certainly not born with the guilt of treachery upon his baby soul. When his mother looked the love light into his eyes in his young and tender years, she saw no treachery there. No more was he a traitor in the early days of his fellowship with Jesus. I know that there are those who say that he was a devil from the beginning. But the Scriptures make no such assertion. In John 6:70 Jesus says, "Have I not chosen you Twelve, and one of you is a devil?" The real meaning of this latter clause is: "One of you is devilish." So spoke Jesus of Judas one year before the betrayal. At that time Judas was facing in the wrong direction. But even then Jesus does not mean to say that he is wholly bad. Judas never became wholly bad. The fact that his ghastly deed filled him with such utter horror shows that there was still much good in him. A man entirely dead to goodness would not have acted as did Judas.

When Jesus therefore said that Judas was devilish, He was only saying what we often say about one another. His criticism was certainly no sharper than that He spoke personally to Simon Peter. This disciple had just risen to great heights. He had said to Jesus, "Thou art the Christ, the Son of the living God." The Master had replied with great enthusiasm, "Blessed art thou; for flesh and blood hath not revealed it unto thee, but my Father who is in heaven." But a moment later, when this same disciple was warning his Master against accepting the Cross, when he was saying, "Be it far from me, Lord," Jesus turned upon him and said, "Get thee behind me, Satan." it was a sharp and cutting word. But it did not mean that Simon was wholly bad. No more does the Master's sharp word about Judas mean that he is beyond hope. Judas became a traitor, but he was not so from the beginning.

3. I think we can only assume that Judas was not always a traitor, but that he was at one time a loyal friend. For this view there are certain arguments that are very convincing.

First, there is the fact that Judas was a disciple of Jesus. He began to follow the Master before he was chosen as an apostle. He followed Jesus of his own choice. How these two met we are not told. But one day they stood face to face. One day they looked into each other's eyes. Perhaps Judas had stood on the fringe of a crowd and heard this strange Prophet speak. He had heard him say, "If any man will come after me, let him deny himself." The conditions seemed hard to one like Judas, who was evidently a lover of money. But in spite of that fact, Judas forsook his business to become a disciple. This amazing Man cast a spell over him that he found impossible to resist.

There are those who suggest that while Judas became a disciple he did so from mixed motives. He was not altogether unselfish. He was not seeing eye to eye with his Lord. Granted. But if we go into the realm of motives, who can stand? Certainly not ourselves, certainly not the fellow-disciples of Judas. James and John came one day, you remember, hiding behind their mother's skirts to ask for positions of particular honor in the Kingdom. Their fellow-disciples were filled with indignation. This was the case, not because they were horrified at their mixed motives, but because, being of mixed motives themselves, they were grasping for the same prize that was being sought by James and John. I believe that Judas was at one time friendly, because of his own choice he became a follower of Jesus.

Second, I believe that Judas was at one time a friend, not only because he chose to follow the Master, but because that Master chose him to be an apostle. Jesus did not have to choose him. There were others, some of them quite worthy, whom he might have selected in the place of this man. Why then did He choose him? I am sure that He did not choose him because he was a rascal. A good man does not choose his closest friends on that basis. No more did He choose him because He saw that he was to be a traitor. He chose him as He chose the other disciples, because he was a man of fine possibilities. He chose him because he had in him the making of a great servant and a great saint.

Finally, I think that we may be sure that Judas was at one time a friend because he was so regarded by his fellow-disciples. They trusted him sufficiently to make him the treasurer of the group. When their Master sent them upon a mission, it is evident that he did his work as well as the rest. If this had not been the case, the Evangelists would doubtless have recorded the fact. They would also, in all probability, have called attention to any indications of treachery if they had known such. But Judas was never suspected. Even at their last meal, when the Master said, "One of you shall betray me," not one looked accusingly at Judas. No one said, "Thou art the man." But with a humility that did not always characterize them, each looked into his own heart and said, "Lord, is it I?" All these reasons tend to prove that Judas was once a loyal friend.

How Then Did Judas Become a Traitor?

There are those who say that Judas was not in reality a treacherous man at all. They affirm that he was only a mistaken man. They believe that, in spite of his seemingly heartless conduct, he deeply loved Jesus. Not only so, but that he trusted him with a faith more daring than that of any of his fellow-disciples. They declare that he believed in Jesus with such absolute conviction that he was sure that, once it became necessary, the Master would assert His power and set up His kingdom. In this faith, these affirm, Judas decided to put his Lord on the spot. He determined to create for Him a situation where He must exercise His power and assume His role of conqueror.

Naturally, there is not one of us that would not like to believe this. But the trouble is, there is no evidence of its truth. All the evidence points in the opposite direction. The Evangelists never speak of Judas as merely a misguided and mistaken man, but always as a deliberately treacherous man. What is more convincing still, Jesus Himself, whose loving eye always saw the best, makes no excuse for Judas. This Man who apologized for the soldiers who murdered Him, who threw about them "the sheltering folds of a protecting prayer," "Father, forgive them, for they know not what they do," has no word of excuse for the Traitor. He does not regard him as a man who through misguided zeal did a foolish thing, but as one who through wickedness of heart did a treacherous and devilish thing.

How then may we explain Judas? Of course, a full explanation is impossible. We can only guess. Of this we may be sure, there came a day when this follower of Jesus began to face away from Him. Judas at some time or another took a false step, and began to travel in the wrong direction. This seemed a small matter at the time, but its end was tragic. I have reminded you before that the direction in which we are traveling is the most important fact about any of us. What we are is of importance, but what we are becoming is of far greater importance. If we are facing in the right direction there is no telling how Christlike we may become, for we have a whole eternity in which to climb. If we are facing in the wrong direction, ever so slightly, there is no telling to what depths we may descend. Judas for some reason took a wrong direction.

As to how he took this false step, we cannot be sure.

Judas was the only disciple who was not a Galilean. That, in itself, offered a soil in which the rank weeds of jealousy might grow. Then one day it became clear to Judas that all the apostles did not share equally in the Master's confidence. Jesus was taking certain ones into an inner circle of friendship. This inner circle was composed of blundering Simon and of hot-hearted James and John. Judas, who was perhaps one of the brightest and best trained men of the group, Judas, who thought well of himself, was not included. In all probability this was a keen disappointment to Judas. Not only so, but it doubtless aroused in him a resentment that grew more bitter with the passing of the days.

This resentment was further increased by the fact that matters were not turning out as Judas had hoped. When he began to follow Jesus, he was sure that the Master was going to establish a temporal and earthly kingdom. That faith he shared along with all the other disciples. Here was a Man who was going to set His people free. He was going to enable His nation to put its foot upon the neck of its foes, to conquer as it had been conquered. But here again he met disappointment. When the Master made His triumphal entry into Jerusalem, when things seemed ripe for a decisive blow, He did nothing more aggressive than weep over the city He should have captured. "Maybe," thought Judas, "He is not to be a conqueror after all."

Thus disappointed in his own personal advancement and in the prospects of a worldly kingdom, Judas had perhaps decided to get out of the mad adventure what little he could. Therefore he began to steal from the common purse. Of course he did not call it stealing. At first he told himself that he would replace the money some day. Then he told himself that what he took was a part payment of his legitimate salary. He was doing most of the work. Besides, the money he took was trifling in proportion to what he could have made had he not given up his business to set out on this wild-goose chase.

While Judas was soothing his conscience by soft lies, while he was deceiving his fellow-disciples, he realized that there was One that he was not deceiving. He felt that Jesus knew him for what he was. He saw disappointment and grief in those kindly eyes that read the very secrets of his soul. Thus he found himself vastly uncomfortable, even wretched in the presence of the Master whose fellowship had once been his comfort and joy. Judas put the blame for this change, not on himself, but on Jesus. Therefore, he came to hate this one-time Friend with a deadly hatred. So intense was his hatred that at last he said to the enemies of Jesus, "What will you give me, and I will deliver him to you?"

What was the price? Thirty pieces of silver. What a trifling sum! It was the price of a slave. No doubt Judas expected far more, but his seducers had him at their mercy. He had betrayed himself into their hands, and there was no going back. Therefore, he took the money because thirty pieces of silver was thirty pieces of silver. But greed was not his primary motive for betraying Jesus. Had such been the case he would not have kissed Him. That kiss was more than a finger pointing the Master out to His foes. "He kissed him lavishly," says Mark. There was venom in those kisses. Jealous, disappointed, greedy Judas had come so to hate the Man that he once loved, that he could betray Him with a kiss.

Three Words to Be Noticed Briefly

What can we say of the destiny of this pathetic man? On this subject the Bible is tenderly reticent. But there are three words that we may notice briefly.

1. There is the word of Simon Peter. He tells us that Judas went to his own place. That is delicately stated. He does not affirm that this false friend plunged into the eternal night. He only says that he went out to meet the destiny that he had prepared for himself. We enter the door, each of us, for which we are ready. If we prepare ourselves for the companionship of the holiest and best, into that companionship we shall surely go. If we prepare ourselves for the companionship of those who hate the best and love the worst, even into that companionship we shall go also. We go each to his own place. So it was with

Judas. Wherever traitors are at home, there we may expect to find this man.

2. Then there is the word of Jesus. What did Jesus think of the destiny of this false friend? Before the betrayal Jesus knew that Judas was not His friend. But He refused to dismiss him. He knew that if love and patience could not save him, ostracism and indifference would surely fail. But Judas made it impossible for the Master to realize His holy purpose for him. Therefore, in His last prayer Jesus says this revealing word: "Those that thou hast given me I have kept, and none of them is lost, but the son of perdition." "The son of perdition"—that is Judas. And Jesus says with infinite heartache, "I have lost him." There can be no more tragic word than that.

3. Finally, there is the verdict of Judas himself. After this kiss, Judas expected to go his way. But this he cannot do. A fatal fascination draws him to the trial. There he hears the Man that he has betrayed sentenced to death. Then a terrible reaction sets in. It is awful to think of the suffering of this desperate man. The very flames of hell are kindled in his heart. Infinitely the most awful hour of his life is upon him. He has needed help before, but never has his need been so crushing as now.

Where does he turn in his hour of need? That is a searching question. The answer to that will give us a look into the very heart of the man. Where do we go when the skies are black, and when life for us has fallen into ruins? We seek help from varied sources. Some turn to drink. Some turn to God. But Judas in this hour of need turns, not to Jesus, but to the heartless devils that have wrecked him. I can conceive of no more revealing nor tragic fact than that. It shows us the effect of Judas' sin upon himself. It has so blinded him to the mercy and goodness of Jesus that at his blackest hour he sees more hope in the worst of men than in Love Incarnate. There can be no hotter hell than that. And this blindness is a danger that threatens, not Judas alone, but every one of us. We can refuse to see until our eyes go out.

NOTES

Judas Iscariot: A Study of Character

Joseph Parker (1830–1902) was one of England's most popular preachers. Largely self-educated, Parker had pulpit gifts that soon moved him into leadership among the Congregationalists. He was a fearless and imaginative preacher who attracted both common people and the aristocracy, and he was particularly a "man's preacher." His *People Bible* is a collection of the shorthand reports of the sermons and prayers Parker delivered as he preached through the entire Bible in seven years (1884–91). He pastored the Poultry Church, London, later called The City Temple, from 1869 until his death.

This sermon is taken from *The Ark of God*, published in 1877 by S. W. Partridge and Co., London. It is also found in Volume 21 of *The People's Bible*, p. 292ff.

Joseph Parker

4

JUDAS ISCARIOT: A STUDY OF CHARACTER

IT WILL HELP ME very greatly in my delicate work of examining the character of the betrayer of our Lord if there be an understanding between us that it is not presumptuously supposed on either side that every difficulty can be explained, and that perfect unanimity can be secured on every point; and especially if it be further understood that my object is not to set up or defend any theory about Judas Iscariot, but solemnly to inquire whether his character was so absolutely unlike everything we know of human nature as to give us no help in the deeper understanding of our own; or whether there was not even in Judas something that, at its very worst, was only an exaggeration of elements or forces that may possibly be in everyone of us.

We always think of him as a monster; but what if we ourselves be—at least in possibility—as monstrous and as vile? Let us go carefully through his history, and see. My purpose is to cut a path as straight as I may be able to go, through the entangled and thorny jungle of texts which make up the history of Iscariot; I propose to stop here and there on the road, that we may get new views and breathe perhaps an uncongenial air; and though we may differ somewhat as to the distance and form of passing objects, I am quite sure that when we get out again into the common highways we shall resume our unanimity, and find it nonetheless entire and cordial because of what we have seen on the unaccustomed and perilous way. First of all, then, let us try to get a clear knowledge of the character of Judas Iscariot, the disciple, and apostle, and betrayer, of the Son of God.

Expository

"Have not I chosen you twelve, and one of you is a devil?" (John 6:70). Who, then, will say that the men with whom Christ began His new kingdom were more than men—not bone of our bone and flesh of our flesh, but a princely sort, specially created and quite away from the common herd in sympathy and aim? He chose twelve men who fairly represented human nature in its best and worst aspects—they represented gentleness, ardor, domesticity, enterprise, timidity, courage—and one of them was a devil. Not a devil in the sense of being something else than human. Judas was a man like the others, but in him there was a preeminent capacity for plotting and attempting the foulest mischief.

We are certainly not to understand that our Lord chose twelve men who, with one exception, were converted, intelligent, sanctified, and perfect; nor is it by any means certain that our Lord chose even the most intellectual and influential men that it was possible for Him to draw into His service. I do not know that we are entitled to regard the Apostles as in all respects the twelve best men of their day; but I think we may justly look upon them as an almost complete representation of all sides of human nature. And as such they utterly destroy the theory that they were but a coterie—men of one mean stamp, without individuality, force, emphasis, or self-assertion; padding, not men; mere shadows of a crafty empiric, and not to be counted as men.

On the contrary, this was a representative discipleship; we were all in that elect band; the kingdom of God, as declared in Christ Jesus, would work upon each according to his own nature, and would reveal every man to himself. A very wonderful and instructive thing is this, that Jesus Christ did not point out the supremely wicked man, but merely said, "One of you is a devil." Thus a spirit of self-suspicion was excited in the whole number, culminating in the mournful "Is it I?" of the Last Supper: and truly it is better for us not to know which is the worst man in the church—to know only that judgment will begin at the house of God, and to be wondering whether that judgment will take most effect upon ourselves.

No man fully knows *himself.* Jesus Christ would seem to be saying to us—At this moment you appear to be a child of God: you are reverent, charitable, well-disposed; you have a place in My visible kingdom—even a prominent place in the pulpit, on the platform, at the desk, in the office; appearances are wholly and strongly in your favor, yet, little as you suspect it, deep under all these things lies an undiscovered *self*—a very devil, it may be; so that even *you*, now loud in your loyalty and zealous beyond all others in pompous diligence, may in the long run turn around upon your Lord and thrust a spear into His heart!

Can it be that the foremost sometimes stumble? Do the strong cedars fall? May the very star of the morning drop from the gate of heaven? Let the veteran, the leader, the hoary Nestor, the soldier valiant beyond all others, say, "Lord, is it I?" Which of us can positively separate himself from Judas Iscariot and honestly say—His was a kind of human nature different from mine? I dare not do so. In the betrayer I would have every man see a *possibility* of himself—himself it may be, magnified in hideous and revolting exaggeration, yet part of the same earth heaved, in the case of Judas, into a great hill by fierce heat, but on exactly the same plane as the coldest dust that lies miles below its elevation. Iscariot's was a human sin rather than a merely personal crime. Individually I did not sin in Eden, but humanly I did; personally I did not covenant for the betrayal of my Lord, but morally I did—I denied Him, and betrayed Him, and spat upon Him, and pierced Him; and He loved me and gave Himself for me!

Of course the question will arise, Why did our Lord choose a man whom He knew to be a devil? A hard question; but there is a harder still—Why did Jesus choose you? Could you ever make out *that* mystery? Was it because of your respectability? Was it because of the desirableness of your companionship? Was it because of the utter absence of all devilishness in your nature? What if Judas did for you what you were only too timid to do for yourself? The Incarnation with a view to human redemption, is the supreme mystery; in comparison with that, every other difficulty is as a molehill to a mountain. In your heart of hearts are you saying, "If this man were a prophet, he would know what manner of man this Judas is, for he is a sinner"? O self-contented Simon, presently the Lord will have somewhat to say to you, and His parable will smite you like a sword.

"The Son of man goeth as it is written of him: but woe unto that man by whom the Son of man is betrayed!" (Matt. 26:24). I think we shall miss the true meaning and pathos of this passage if we regard it merely as the exclamation of a man who was worsted for the moment by superior strength, but who would get the upper hand by-and-by, and then avenge his humiliation. These words might have been uttered with tears of the heart—Woe will be the portion of that man who betrays me; yes, woe upon woe, even to remorse and agony and death; the chief of sinners, he will also be chief of sufferers; when he sees the full meaning of what he has done, he will sink under the intolerable shame, he will give blood for blood, and be glad to find solace in death.

And if our hearts be moved at all to pitifulness in the review of this case, may we not find somewhat of a redeeming feature in the capacity for suffering so deep and terrible? Shall we be stretching the law of mercy unduly if we see in this self-torment a faint light on the skirts of an appalling cloud? I do not find that Judas professed or manifested any joy in his grim labor; there is no sound of revel or mad hilarity in all the tragic movement; on the contrary, there is a significant absence, so far as we can judge from the narrative, of all the excitement needful for nerving the mischievous man to work out purposes which he knows to be wholly evil. All the while, Judas would seem to be under a cloud, to be advancing stealthily rather than boisterously; he was no excited Belshazzar whose brain was aflame with excess of wine—though he, too, trembled as if the mystic hand were writing letters of doom upon the old familiar scenes: so excited is he that a word will send him reeling backward to the ground, and if he do not his work "quickly" he will become sick with fear and be incapable of action; as it is, he has only bargained to "kiss" the Victim, not to clutch Him with a ruffian's grasp. Then came the intolerable woe!

This great law is at work upon our lives today. Woe to the unfaithful pastor; woe to the negligent steward; woe to the betrayer of sacred interests; woe to them that call evil good and good evil—to all such be woe; not only the woe of outward judgment—divine and inexorable—but that, if may be, still keener, sadder woe of self-contempt and self-damnation. With such sorrow no stranger may intermeddle. The lesson to ourselves would seem to be this—Do not regard divine judgment merely as measure for measure in relation to your sin—that is to say, so much penalty for so much guilt. It is more than that—it is a quickening of the man into holy resentment against himself, an arming of the conscience against the whole life, a subjective controversy which will not be lulled into unrighteous peace, but will rage wrathfully and implacably until there shall come repentance to life or remorse to death.

Shall I startle you if I say that there is a still more terrible state than that of such anguish as Iscariot's? To have worn out the moral sense, to have become incapable of pain, to have the conscience seared as with a hot iron, to be "past feeling"—*that* is the consummation of wickedness. That there is a judicial and outward infliction of pain on account of sin, is of course undoubted; but while that outward judgment may actually harden the sinner, the bitter woe which comes of a true estimate of sin and of genuine contrition for its enormity may work out a repentance not to be repented of. If, then, any man is suffering the pain of just self-condemnation on account of sin; if any man's conscience is now rising mightily against him and threatening to tear him in pieces before the Lord, because of secret lapses or unholy betrayals, because of long-sustained hypocrisy or self-seeking faithlessness, I will not hurriedly seek to ease the healthy pain; the fire will work to his purification, and the Refiner will lose nothing of the gold. But if any man, how eminent soever in ecclesiastical position, knows that he has betrayed the Lord, and conceals under a fair exterior all that Ezekiel saw in the chamber of imagery, and is as a brazen wall against every appeal—hard, tearless, impenetrable, unresponsive—I do not hesitate to say that I would rather be numbered with Judas than with that man.

"It had been good for that man if he had not been born" (Matt. 26:24). Then why was he born? is the question, not of impatient ignorance only, but of a certain moral instinct which God never fails to respect throughout the whole of His relationship with mankind, and which He will undoubtedly honor in this instance. Take the case as it is ordinarily put: Judas, like the rest of us, had no control over his own birth; he found himself in a world in whose formation he had no share; he was born under circumstances which, as to their literal and local bearing, can never be repeated in all the ages of time.

So far as we can gather from the narrative, Jesus spoke to him no word of sympathy, never drew him aside, as He drew Peter, to tell him of preventing prayer, but to all appearance left him to be the blind and helpless instrument of the devil, and then said, "It had been good for that man if he had not been born." This cannot be the full meaning of the words. Instantly we repeat the profound inquiry of Abram, "Shall not the Judge of all the earth do right?" He may, and must, transcend our understanding; He will, by the very nature of the case, dazzle and confound our imagination by the unsuspected riches and glory of His many mansions; but He must not trouble our sense of *right* if He would retain our homage and our love.

Personally, I can have no share in the piety that can see any man condemned under such circumstances as have just been described; it is not enough to tell me that it is some other man and not myself who suffers—a suggestion ineffably mean even if it were true; but it is *not* true; I *do* suffer: a tremendous strain is put upon my sensibilities, and I cannot, without anguish, see any man arbitrarily driven into hell. Upon his face, writhing in unutterable torture, is written this appeal, "Can you see me, bone of your bone and flesh of your flesh, thus treated, weighed down, crushed, damned, by a power I am utterly unable either to placate or resist!" That man may be my own father, my own child, my most familiar friend; and though he be a stranger, of name unknown, he has at all events the claim of our common humanity upon me. I have purposely put the case in this strong way, that I may say with the more emphasis that I see no such method of government revealed in the narrative now under consideration. If I saw anything like it in any part of the Word of God, I should say, "My understanding is at fault, not God's justice; from what I know of His method within the scope of my own life, I know and am sure that righteousness and judgment are the habitation of His throne, and that His mercy endureth forever." I see things that are mysterious, incomprehensible, baffling; I come upon Scriptures which utterly defy all scholars and interpreters; but this is the confidence that I have—*the Judge of all the earth will do right.*"

As to the particular expression in the text, two things may be said:

First, it is well known that the Jews were in the habit of saying, "It had been good for that man had he not been born,"—it was a common expression of the day, in speaking of transgressors, and did not by any means imply a belief in the final destruction or damnation of the person spoken of.

Secondly, *this passage has again and again exactly expressed our own feeling in many crises of our own life*: it must be forever true that non-existence is better than sinfulness. When the lie was on our lips, when part of the price was laid down as the whole, when we dishonored the vow we made in secret with God, when we rolled iniquity under our tongue as a sweet morsel—at *that* time it had been good for us if we had not been born.

Such, indeed, is the only form of words equal to the gravity of the occasion; better we say, again and again, not to have been born than to have done this; if this be the end of our being, then has our life been a great failure and a mortal pain. I hold that these words were spoken not so much of Judas the *man* as of Judas the *sinner*, and that consequently they apply to all evil-doers throughout all generations, and are in reality the most tender and pathetic admonition which even Christ could address to the slaves of sin.

We may get some light upon this expression by considering the fact that "it repented the Lord that He had made man." In studying all such passages we must have regard to the order of time. St. Paul said, "If in this life only we have hope, we are of all men most miserable." So, if we break off our own life at certain points, we shall say the same thing of ourselves; and if we interrupt human history, so that one fact shall not be allowed to explain another, it would be easy to find sections which would prove alike the disorder and malignity of the Divine government.

We know what this means in some of the works of our own hands. Thus, for example: You undertook to build a house for the Lord, and your heart was full of joy as you saw the sacred walls rising in your hopeful dreams; but when you came to work out your purpose, you came upon difficulty after difficulty—promises were broken, contracts were trifled with, the very stars in their courses seemed to fight against you, and at length, after many disappointments and exasperations, you said, "It repents me; it gives me pain, it grieves me, that I began this house." Such is the exact state of your feeling at that particular moment. But other influences were brought to bear upon the situation, resources equal to the difficulty were developed, and when the roof covered the walls, and the spire shot up into the clouds, you forget your pains and tears in a great satisfaction. You will say that God foresaw all the difficulty of building the living temple of manhood, that the whole case was clearly before Him from eternity; that is, of course, true; but the pain of ingratitude is nonetheless keen because the ingratitude itself was foreknown.

Take the case of Jesus Christ, God manifest in the flesh, as an illustration. He foresaw all the triumphs of His cross—all heaven thronged with innumerable multitudes out of every kindred and people and tongue—yet

He prayed that the cup might pass from Him, and He needed an angel to help Him in the time of His soul's sorrow. In magnifying God's omniscience we must not overlook God's love; nothing, indeed, could surprise His foreknowledge, yet it grieved Him at the heart that He had made man; and He called upon the heavens to hear and upon the earth to be astonished, because His children had rebelled against Him!

"This he said, not that he cared for the poor, but because he was a thief and had the bag, and bare what was put therein" (John 12:6). It is more to the credit of the apostles themselves that this should be regarded as an afterthought than as an undoubted conviction, or an established fact, at the time that Judas sat with them at the Paschal Supper, or even at the time that he asked why the ointment was not sold for the benefit of the poor. This is more evident from the fact that the writer indicates Judas as the betrayer, whereas at the moment of the test his identity was not established. There is no mystery about the insertion of this explanatory suggestion, for we all know how easy it is *after* a character has fully revealed itself to go back upon its separate acts and account for them by their proper motives—motives unknown at the time of the action, but plainly proved by subsequent revelations of character. This was probably the case in the instance before us: else why did the disciples allow Judas to keep the bag? Why did they not humble and exhaust him by an incessant protest against his dishonesty? And why did not our Lord, instead of mildly expostulating, say to Judas as He once said to Peter, "Get thee behind me, Satan"?

Here, then, is a great law within whose operation we ourselves may be brought—the law of reading the part in the light of the whole, and of judging the isolated act by the standard of the complete character. Illustrations of the working of this law will occur to you instantly. Let a man eventually reveal himself as having unworthily filled prominent positions in the church—let his character be proved to have been corrupt, and then see what light is thrown upon words and deeds which at the time were not fully understood. How abundant then will be such expressions—these in recounting his utterances:

"He advised prudence and care and very great caution in working out church plans; he counseled concentration; he deprecated romantic schemes: this he did (as we *now* can see), not that he was a lover of Prudence or a worshiper of Wisdom, but because he was a thief, and he feared that bold and noble schemes would shame him into reluctant generosity."

"He urged that the church should be built with the least possible decoration or ornament; he spoke strongly against colored glass and elaborate enrichment: and this he did (as we can *now* see), not that he was devoted to Simplicity or absorbed in spiritual aspiration, but because he was a thief, and feared that every block of polished marble would increase the sum which his respectability would be expected to subscribe."

"He denounced all heretical tendencies in the Christian ministry; he knew heterodoxy afar off; he never ceased to declare himself in favor of what he supposed to be the Puritan theology: and this he did, not that in his heart of hearts he cared for the conservation of orthodoxy, but because he was a thief, and had a felonious intent upon the reputation of independent thinkers whose shoelaces he was not worthy to unloose."

All this comes out *after* a man has revealed himself as Judas did. But let me also say that the "thief" may be dictating our speech even when we least suspect it, certainly where there may never be such a disclosure as there was in the case of Judas. There are conditions under which we hardly know what influence it is that colors our judgment and suggests our course—may it not be the "thief" that underlies our consciousness, and so cunningly touches our life as never to excite our suspicion or our fear? We know how subtle are the workings of self-deception, and perhaps even the godliest of us would be surprised to know exactly the inspiration of some of our most fervent speeches—surprised to find that though the outward orator seemed to be an earnest man, the inner and invisible speaker is the "thief" that prompted Judas!

Who, then, can stand before the Lord, or be easy in the presence of His holy law? It is under such inquiries that the strongest man quails, and that the swiftest of God's messengers humbly prays, "Enter not into judgment with thy servant, O Lord; for in thy sight shall no flesh living be justified."

"Then one of the twelve, called Judas Iscariot, went unto the chief priests, And said unto them, What will ye give me, and I will deliver him unto you?" (Matt. 26:14–15). Why should there have been any bargaining, or why should there have been any difficulty about the arrest of Christ? We must look to an earlier verse for the solution. The chief priests, the scribes, and the elders, had met for consultation in the palace of the high priest, Caiaphas, and the principal question was, not how they might take Jesus, but how they might take Him by subtilty, by craft, deceit, guile, as if they would have secretly murdered Him if they could—murdered Him in the darkness, and in the morning have wiped their mouths as innocent men! Judas would appear to have gone to them secretly, and offered himself as one who knew the haunts and times and methods of Christ; and in doing so he showed the weak and vicious side of his nature, his covetousness, his greed, his love of money—and herein his guilt seems to culminate in an aggravation infernal and unpardonable.

But are we ourselves verily clear in this matter? Are we not every day selling Christ to the highest bidder? When we stifle our convictions lest we should lose a morsel of bread; when we are dumb in the presence of the enemy lest our words should be followed by loss of domestic comfort or personal honor; when we soften our speech, or hide the Cross, or join in ungodly laughter that we may avoid an ungodly sneer, we are doing in our own way the very thing which we rightly condemn in the character of Judas.

"Then Judas which had betrayed him, when he saw that he was condemned, repented himself and brought again the thirty pieces of silver to the chief priests and elders, Saying, I have sinned in that I have betrayed the innocent blood: . . . And he cast down the silver pieces in

the temple, and departed, and went and hanged himself"
(Matt. 27:3–5). Is there not a tone in these words with
which we are familiar? Is there not, indeed, something of
our own voice in this mournful story? Let us look at it
carefully:

"When he *saw*"—that, at least, is familiar! Not until
our actions are set a little off do we see all their relations
and all their meaning; in their progress we are too near
them to get their full effect; if we take but one step back
we shall be affrighted by the very actions of which the
doing gave us a kind of frenzied joy. We make our own
ghosts. We shut the eyes of our minds while we are doing
certain things; and when the last touch is given to the
deed, we are taught by the bitterness of experience that
Temptation destroys our sight and that Guilt restores it.
Recall the case of Adam and Eve—"And the eyes of them
both were opened"! Very short and cloudy is the sight of
the body: how keen, how piercing, is the sight of a self-
convicted soul! Before that discerning vision the air is full
of eyes, and the clearest of all days is dark with menaces
and gathering thunders.

"When he saw that he was *condemned.*" At that moment the surprise of Judas himself was supreme and
unutterable: evidently he did not expect that this catastrophe would supervene. He may, indeed, have said to
himself—as a man of inventive and daring mind would be
likely to say—I am quite sure, from what I have seen of
His miracles, that He will prove Himself more than a
match for all His enemies; He has done so before, and He
will do it again. They said they would cast Him down
from the brow of the hill, but He went through the midst
of them like a beam of light, and when they took up
stones to stone Him, their hands were held fast by that
strong will of His. He has provoked them to their face,
heaped up all their sins before them, taunted and goaded
them to madness, and yet He held them in check and
played with them as He listed; it will be so again. Besides, He may just want a plan like mine to bring things
to a point; I will put Him into the hands of these men,
then will He shake them off, proclaim His kingdom, drive

away the spoiler from the land of the Hebrews, and we shall come into the enjoyment of our promised reward. Judas may not have used these words, but in effect they are being used by sinners every day! This is the universal tongue of self-deception, varying a little, it may be, in the accent, but in substance the same all the world over; a putting of one thing against another, a balancing of probabilities, an exercise of self-outwitting cunning; a secret hope that something can be snatched out of the fire, and that the flames can be subdued without undue damage— this is the method of sinfulness of heart, a method confounded every day by the hand of God, yet every day coming up again to fresh attempts and renewed humiliations.

"When he saw that he was condemned he *repented* himself." Is there not hope of a man who is capable of any degree of repentance, even when repentance takes upon itself the darker shade of horror and remorse? I know what the word is which is translated "repented," and I remember with joy that it is the word which is used of the sin who said he would not go, and afterward repented and went; it is the word which Paul used of himself on one occasion in writing to the Corinthians. But even if the word be rendered "was filled with remorse and shame and despair," I should say, "So much the better for Judas." Under such circumstances I should have more hope of a man who had absolutely no hope of himself, than of a man who could sufficiently control himself to think that even such a sin—infinite in wickedness as it must have appeared to his own mind—could ever be forgiven. It is easy for us who never experienced the agony to say what Judas ought to have done: how he ought to have wept and prayed and sought forgiveness as we now should seek it— we cannot intermeddle with his sorrow, nor ought we harshly to judge the method of his vengeance.

"*I have sinned in that I have betrayed the innocent blood.*" Not, "I was hurried into this by others"; not, "Others are as much to blame as I am"; but, "I did it, and I alone." Not, "I have made a mistake"; not, "This is a great error on my part"; but, "I have sinned"—the very word

which he might have heard in his Lord's parable of the
Prodigal Son—the word which our Father in heaven de-
lights to hear! "If we confess our sins, He is faithful and
just to forgive us our sins, for His mercy endureth forever." "If thy brother turn again, saying, I repent, forgive
him"—Judas repented himself! "How often shall I forgive
him. Seven times. Seventy times seven"! And shall I forgive him the less because his repentance has deepened
into remorse, and he has lost all hope of himself? Surely
the more on that very account. And if he slay himself
because of his sin against me? Then must I think of him
with still more tender pity, nor cloud his memory with a
single suspicion.

And here let me say, as to the spiritual application of
this matter, I have no faith in the moral value of fine-
drawn distinctions between repentance and despair; my
belief is that until we reach the point of self-despair as to
our sin against Christ, we can never know the true meaning or realize the true joy of repentance. That Judas should
have slain himself with his own hand is, in my view of the
case, wholly in his favor. It must have appeared to him,
indeed, to be the only course open to him; floods of tears
he could never set against the blood of an innocent man;
to cry and moan and weep bitterly, would be just to aggravate the appalling crime. With a stronger light beating
on our life than ever Judas was permitted to enjoy, guarded
by all the restraints of Christian civilization, living under
the ministry of the Holy Spirit, we are by so much unable
to sympathize with the intolerable horror which destroyed
the self-control of the Betrayer of our Lord.

So far as I can think myself back into the mental condition of Judas, his suicide seems to me to be the proper
completion of his insufferable self-reproach. And yet that
self-control was preserved long enough to enable Judas
Iscariot to utter the most effective and precious eulogy
ever pronounced upon the character of Jesus Christ. How
brief, how simple, how complete—"innocent blood"! If the
proper interpretation of words is to be found, as it undoubtedly is, in circumstances, then these two words are
fuller in meaning and more tender in pathos than the

most labored encomium could possibly be. Consider the life which preceded these words, and you will see that they may be amplified thus: "I know Jesus better than any of you can know Him; you have only seen Him in public, I have lived with Him in private. I have watched His words as words of man were never watched before. I have heard His speeches meant for His disciples alone. I have seen Him in poverty, weariness, and pain of heart; I have heard His prayers at home. I trusted that it had been He who would have redeemed Israel from patriotic servility. I curse myself, I exonerate Him—His is innocent blood!"

How glad would the Jews have been if Christ had been witnessed against by one of His own disciples! They would have welcomed his evidence; no gold could have adequately paid for testimony so direct and important; and Judas loved gold. Yet the holy truth came uppermost; Judas died not with a lie in his right hand, but with the word of truth upon his lips, and the name of Christ was thus saved from what might have been its deepest wound.

"*Those that thou gavest me I have kept, and none of them is lost, but the son of perdition*" (John 17:12). At the first glance these words would seem to put the fate of Judas Iscariot beyond all controversy, yet further consideration may show how mercy may magnify itself even in this cloud. Judas is called "the son of perdition"; true, and Peter himself was called Satan by the same Lord. And if Judas was "the son of perdition," what does Paul say of all mankind? Does he not say, "We are by nature *the children of wrath*, even as others"? But in this case "the son of perdition" is said to be "lost"; but does the word lost necessarily imply that he was in hell? "We have all erred and strayed like *lost* sheep"; "the Son of man came to seek and to save that which was *lost*"; and, "there is joy in the presence of the angels of God over one sinner that repenteth [Judas repented himself], more than over ninety and nine just persons that need no repentance." It is our joy to believe that wherever repentance is possible, mercy is possible; and it is heaven to us to know that where sin abounded, grace did much more abound. And are we *quite* sure that there is no ray of hope falling upon the repentant and remorseful Judas from such words as these: "And this is the Father's will which hath sent me, that of all which He hath given me [and that He gave him Iscariot is clear from the very passage we are now considering] I should lose nothing, but should raise it up again at the last day" (John 6:39)? But there is still more light to be thrown on this great gloom. Take this passage (John 18:8–9): "Jesus answered, I have told you that I am he if therefore ye seek me, let these go their way; that the saying might be fulfilled which he spake, Of them which thou gavest me I have lost none."

Now suppose that the ruffians had answered, "No, we will not let these go their way; we will slay them with the sword at once"—would it follow that Jesus Christ had *lost* His disciples in the sense of their having been destroyed in unquenchable fire? The suggestion is not to be entertained for a moment, yet this is the very "saying" which is supposed to determine the damnation of Judas! As I read the whole history, I cannot but feel that our Lord was especially wistful that His disciples should *continue* with Him throughout His temptation, should *watch* with Him, that in some way, hardly to be expressed in words, they should help Him by the sympathy of their *presence*—in this sense He was anxious to "lose none"; but He did lose the one into whom Satan had entered, and He refers to him not so much for His own sake as that He may rejoice the more in the constancy of those who remained. But the whole reference, as it seems to me, is not to the final and eternal state of men in the unseen world, but to continuance and steadfastness in relation to a given crisis.

"This ministry and apostleship, from which Judas by transgression fell, that he might go to his own place" (Acts 1:25). One reputable scholar has suggested that the words "go to his own place" may refer to Matthias, and not to Judas; but the suggestion does not commend itself to my judgment. I think we should lose a good deal by accepting this interpretation. I hold that this is an instance of exquisite delicacy on the part of Peter: no judgment is pronounced; the fall is spoken of only as official and as

involving official results, and the sinner himself is left in the hands of God. It is in this spirit that Peter speaks of Judas:

> Owning his weakness,
> His evil behavior,
> And leaving with meekness
> His sins to his Savior.

Practical

Such a study as this can hardly fail to be fruitful of suggestion to the nominal followers of Christ in all ages. What are its lessons to ourselves—to ourselves as Christians, ministers, office-bearers, and stewards of heavenly mysteries?

1. Our first lesson will be found in the fact that when our Lord said to His disciples, "One of you shall betray me," every one of them began to say, "Is it I?" Instead of being shocked even to indignation, each of the disciples put it to himself as a *possibility*; "it *may* be I; Lord, *is* it I?" This is the right spirit in which to hold all our privileges. We should regard it as a *possibility* that the strongest may fall, and even the oldest may betray His trust. "Let him that thinketh he standeth take heed lest he fall."

Do you suppose that there was but *one* betrayal of the Lord once for all, and that the infamous crime can never be repeated? "I tell you, nay"! There are predictions yet to be realized—"There shall be false teachers among you, who privily shall bring in damnable heresies, even denying the Lord that bought them";—"Lord, is it I?" It shall surely be more tolerable for Judas Iscariot in the day of judgment than for that man! Living in the light of gospel day; professing to have received the Holy Spirit; ordained as a minister of the Cross; holding office in the Christian church—"it is impossible for those who were once enlightened, and have tasted of the heavenly gift, and were made partakers of the Holy Spirit, and have tasted the good Word of God, and the powers of the world to come, if they shall fall away, to renew them again to repentance;

seeing that they crucify to themselves the Son of God afresh, and put Him to an open shame." "Lord, is it I?"

"In the last days perilous times shall come; men shall be traitors"—"Lord, is it I?" Governing our life by this self-misgiving spirit, not thinking all men sinful but ourselves, we shall be saved from the boastfulness which is practical blasphemy, and our energy shall be kept from fanaticism by the chastening influence of self-doubt. Looking upon all the mighty men who have made shipwreck of faith and a good conscience—Adam, Saul, Solomon, Judas—let us be careful lest after having preached to others we ourselves should be cast away.

It is true that we cannot repeat the literal crime of Judas, but there are greater enormities than his! We can outdo Judas in sin! "Whosoever speaketh a word against the Son of man it shall be forgiven him, but whosoever speaketh against the Holy Spirit it shall not be forgiven him, neither in this world, nor in the world to come" (Matt. 12:32). We cannot sell the body, but we can grieve the Spirit! There can be no more covenanting over the Lord's bones, but we can plunge a keener spear into His heart than that which drew forth blood and water from His side; we cannot nail Him to the accursed tree, but we can pierce Him through with many sorrows.

Judas died by the vengeance of his own hand; of how much sorer punishment, suppose, shall he be thought worthy, who has done despite to the Spirit of Grace? Judas shall rise in judgment with this generation, and shall condemn it, because when he saw the error of his ways he repented himself, and made restitution of his unholy gains; but we have rolled iniquity under our tongue as a sweet morsel, we have held our places in the sanctuary while our heart has been the habitation of the enemy! It will be a fatal error on our part if we suppose that human iniquity reached its culmination in the sin of Judas, and that after his wickedness all other guilt is contemptible in magnitude and trivial in effect. Jesus Christ teaches another doctrine: He points to a higher crime—that higher crime, the sin against the Holy Spirit, He leaves without specific and curious definition that out of its possibility may come a continual fear, and a perpetual discipline. Grieve not the Holy Spirit of God, whereby you are sealed to the day of redemption!

2. Our second lesson is a caution against mere intellectual sagacity in directing the affairs of the Christian kingdom. It is admitted on all hands that Judas Iscariot was far ahead of the other apostles in many intellectual qualities, yet "Judas by transgression fell." How self-controlled he was, how stealthy was his step, how lingering and watchful his cunning! And if Whately and De Quincey be right in the suggestion that he merely wanted to force the Lord to declare Himself the Prince of princes and make Israel glad by despoiling the oppressor, it discovers the instinct of statesmanship, and shows how his strategic ambition sought to ensnare the Roman fowler in his own net.

Judas is supposed to have reasoned thus with himself: This Jesus is He who will redeem Israel; the whole twelve of us think so; yet He hesitates, for some reason we cannot understand; His power is astounding, His life is noble. This will I do, I will bring things to a crisis by going to the authorities and making them an offer. I believe they will snatch at my proposition, and when they come to work it out He will smite them with His great power, and will avenge the insult by establishing His supremacy as King and Lord of Israel. As a matter of fact we know that this kind of reasoning has played no small part in the history of the church. The spiritual kingdom of Christ has suffered severely at the hands of men who have been proud of their own diplomacy and generalship; men fond of elaborating intricate organizations, of playing one influence against another, and of making up for the slowness of time by dramatic surprises alike of sympathy and collision. It is for this reason that I cannot view without alarm the *possible misuse* of congresses, conferences, unions, and councils: these institutions will only be of real service to the cause of the Cross in proportion as *spiritual* influence is supreme—once let political sagacity, diplomatic ingenuity, and official adroitness in the management of details, become unduly valued, and you change the center of gravity, and bring the church into imminent peril.

Unquestionably human nature loves dexterity and will pay high prices for all kinds of conjuring, and loudly applaud the hero who does apparent impossibilities. From this innate love of mere cleverness may come betrayals, compromises, and casuistries which crucify the Son of God afresh. Judas looked to the end to vindicate if not to sanctify the means; and this is the policy of all dexterous managers, the very soul of Jesuistry, and a chosen instrument of the devil. I do not pray for a leader, fertile in resource, supple and prompt in movement. My prayer is for a man of another stamp, even for an *Inspirer*, who, by the ardor of his holiness, the keenness of his spiritual insight, and the unction of his prayers, shall help us truthward and heavenward. Under his leadership we shall hear no more about secularities and temporalities, but every action—the opening of the doors and the lighting of the lamps of the sanctuary—shall be done by hands which were first outstretched in prayer. Not the crafty Judas, but the loving John will help us best in all our work; not the man inexhaustible in tricks of management, but the man of spiritual intelligence and fervor, will deliver us most successfully in the time of straits and dangers. Managers, leaders, draftsmen, and pioneers, we shall of course never cease to want, and their abilities will always be of high value to every good cause; yet one thing is needful above all others—closeness to the dear Lord, and daily continuance in prayer.

NOTES

Judas Iscariot

J. Stuart Holden (1874-1934), Vicar of St. Paul's Church, Portman Square, London, was an Anglican preacher of great ability. Possessing an engaging personality and persuasive manner, Holden was known on both sides of the Atlantic for his convention ministries. Holden was leader of the Keswick movement for almost 30 years and guided it ably. Skilled as a diagnostician of the deeper spiritual life, he helped guide many in discerning the difference between spurious and genuine faith.

This message on God's mercy is from *The Master and His Men* by J. Stuart Holden, published by Marshall, Morgan and Scott, London, 1953.

J. Stuart Holden

5

JUDAS ISCARIOT

OF ALL THE MEN who came into revealing association
with the Master, Judas Iscariot is perhaps the most
striking and certainly not the least interesting. For while
he began in the clear light of morning to company with
Him and with His, his career ended in the blackness of a
starless midnight. His name stands for perfidy, for
treachery, for the most damning and damnable of all sins—
the betrayal of a trustful friend. So that, even to this day,
to liken a man to Judas is to put the greatest possible
dishonor upon him. Men will consort with flagrantly bad
men, with men whose weakness or whose circumstances,
or both, have brought them within the displeasure of
society and the meshes of the law, and will make
allowances for them and succeed in finding some good in
them. But no man wants to be a friend of a Judas-man!
His is the unforgivable sin. A leprosy of shame clings to
him. Contempt is the only feeling that ordinarily decent
men can have for him. By every rule of human association
he has put himself outside the pale.

Everyone knows that behind the particular act that earned
for him that title of infamy there lies a story of base ingratitude and sly selfishness and slimy falseness, masked by
hateful hypocrisy and nauseating cant. With such evil sig-
nificance has Judas filled a once honorable name! For the
name was not always despised and abhorred—Judas
Maccabeus, for example, was one of the greatest and truest
Hebrew patriots. Judas the brother of Jesus, too, bore the
name without attaching any sinister meaning to it. But this
Judas, one of the Master's chosen men, dragged it in the
mire, degraded it beyond the lowest; until there is no name
so surrounded with loathing. And the mother is not yet born
who would ever allow her child to be christened Judas!

And yet no man in the group had any more promising start than Judas. Although we know nothing of the actual event of his calling by the Master, what experiences led up to it, what influences had been at work urging him to link up with Jesus and the new movement, it is quite evident that Judas was entirely sincere. There is no evidence at all that he was, from the first, a self-seeking hypocrite. Nor that the Master who, it must be remembered, spent a whole night in prayer before choosing the Twelve, had made any mistake in including him. On the contrary, it is fair to assume that he was moved by a blameless and noble enthusiasm when (as a man with some experience of affairs, for was he not made the group treasurer?) he made that renunciation which all must make who would join the Master and which to others must have seemed like madness. Conviction and eager courage voiced a faith which was bright with the bloom of freshness and eagerness. Judas was as much in earnest, and as disinterested, in joining the group as any of the others.

The only handicap upon his intentions was the same handicap which each carried—his own nature, with which constant contact with the Master was calculated to deal effectively, to reduce it from a disability to a positive capacity. In the case of all the others this actually happened. They became increasingly competent for the carrying out of His bidding by becoming increasingly of one mind and purpose with Him. Judas grew steadily worse until in the end "Satan entered into him" through a door which he himself opened! He became blinded to all his vows and recreant to all his experiences and disloyal to all his benefits. He made a calculated bargain with the Master's enemies to betray Him into their power for a paltry price. He feigned a friendship he no longer felt, and actually kissed the Master whose downfall he was profitably assisting in. He became the victim of unavailing remorse and of unsatisfying success; and by his own hand "went to his own place" (to carry out the eternal destiny for which he had fitted himself) unattended except by stinging, scorching, mocking memories and regrets! And of him the Master said: "it had been good for that man had he not been born!"

> For ships sail East, and ships sail West
> On the self-same winds that blow.
> It is not the gale, but the set of the sail
> That determines the way they go!

It's really a terrifying story, for what happened to him might happen to any of us. Privilege evidently does not ensure men against ultimate disaster. The same kind of tragedy may be reforming in any life, as witness the startled question of the other men in the group when the Master said: "One of you shall betray Me"—question which voiced a wholesome misgiving: "Lord, is it I?" Let no one settle down to a self-complacent survey of Judas, as though they themselves are remote from all possibility of such undetected instabilities as brought about his ruin. "Let him that thinketh he standeth take heed lest he fall."

How did it all begin? And how did it go on as it did under the influence and the eye of the Master, and the protective activities of the life of His men together? Well, it all began by Judas failing to make an entire surrender of himself to the Master at the start. He simply didn't leave all when he joined Him. He carried over into the new life part of the old love, which right from the start disputed the Master's absolute rule, and finally repudiated it entirely. Judas was a mercenary-minded man, and always had been; the kind of man of whom it is said "he's keen"—meaning thereby keen on making money. He had what is called "an eye for the main chance," but, like most men of that ilk, he didn't know what the *main chance* really is! He thought it was money and so became "penny-wise and soul-foolish"! And even though he was continually hearing so much from the Master about such folly (hearing without learning!), he let money exercise its fatal charm upon him, until he'd do anything (and anybody!) for it—without it ever dawning upon him that he was vainly trying to do what the Master said was impossible—to serve God and Mammon. All of which is not to suggest that he was a deliberately bad man, only that he was a "double-minded man." He simply did not let his new allegiance dislodge the old supremacy. He did not yield to the Master the whole area of life. He consented (with himself) to be only partly "spiritual"! And the old nature—which is always the battleground of the new life—asserted itself, until Judas just couldn't understand how the Master could be so indifferent to money, and all that it brings, and to rich men whom He seemed to antagonize with so little respect! Until, indeed, he honestly felt that Jesus and His unworldly group really needed someone "with a head on his shoulders" to look after their interests, and actually persuaded himself that he was that heaven-sent protection! As witness, when a poor woman poured her treasured ointment in fragrant devotion upon the Master's feet, his protest: "It might have been sold for 300 pence!"

Slowly and insidiously he came entirely under the power of the thing he really loved most. Temptation made successful appeal to latent cupidity. Zeal for the unselfish ideals of the Master began to flag as greed gradually took over control of his soul. Covetousness got the better of piety. Moral corrosion set in. A few pence, taken now and again from the bag, fed the flame of his money-lust which culminated in his acceptance of the High Priest's thirty pieces of silver. He was overcome just because his allegiance, openly professed, was secretly divided; just because he wasn't wholehearted. Sincere as far as he went, he didn't go far enough! No one suspected him of dishonest action or of disloyal intention. He was certainly able to keep up appearances right to the end. At the Supper, with the thirty pieces of silver in his pocket weighing him down like thirty pieces of lead, he was yet able to sit near enough to the Master to dip his bread into the same dish. And, later, Judas came quite naturally up to Him to give Him the perfidious kiss!

And what about the Master, who knew well what was going on in the soul of the one He had chosen? Did He do nothing to save him from himself? It would seem as though He did everything possible to discover Judas to himself; to draw him out in self-confession of his tendencies and fears, and into closer intimacy with Himself who could have done wonders to help him overcome the money-menace which threatened and ultimately managed to destroy him. Think of the simply tremendous things He said about it—things which could only have concerned Judas, of all the group—about the tragedy of bursting barns and an insecure soul; about the disaster of a world gained and a life lost; about being aware of the blight of covetousness; about the abject folly of laying up for oneself earthly riches. It actually appears as though the Master had had him in mind more than all the rest! Judas must, many a time, have been afraid to catch the Master's eye. And it does not surprise us that, as the end drew near, "Jesus was troubled in spirit" at the thought that one of His men could be treacherous and betray His confidence. One can almost hear Him, in the solitude of His prayer place, repeating the old Psalm: "Mine own familiar friend in whom I trusted, who did eat of my bread hath lifted up his heel against me. We took sweet counsel together and walked in the house of God as friends!" And again turning from this bitterness to His unfailing refuge!

What would not have happened if Judas had only taken his misgivings, in secret, to the Master! If he had just told Him that he had a foe that was too strong for him! If only he had opened his heart as readily to Him as he was opening it to the demon of greed and avarice! But no! He was in love with the foe! His idol had become his ideal! His heart had never been wholly the Master's, and every day its divided, contending loyalties were more evident and more unreconcilable.

Even to the last the Master endeavored to make him face up to himself. At the Table He gives him the sop! In the Garden He calls him "Friend" and does not resist his treacherous kiss! It was a last endeavor to win him back to his first intention! But it failed! The poor, possessed man violently wrenches himself from the kindly grasp of love, and takes the mad plunge! When the raging fever cooled to disillusion and despair, his too-late confession: "I have sinned," completely exonerated the Master! He had done His utmost (and Judas knew it) to save him.

It has been ingeniously suggested that Judas was not

simply out for personal gain in betraying Christ. That he was moved by vehement zeal to force Him to declare Himself a king! That he resented Christ's unbusinesslike way of going about things, and so maneuvered to put Him into a position from which He could only extricate Himself by a spectacular and convincing miracle! That he was merely trying to speed up the establishment of the Kingdom, to the service of which he had pledged himself! It has even been suggested that this idea of his was reinforced by his jealousy of the favored Three—possibly of the entire eleven. They were all Galileans; he was from Kerioth in southeast Judea, a stranger among them and made to feel his position by them! He would establish himself, by a stroke of cleverness, as the Master's truest friend, the leader of the group. All very ingenious, but all such attempts favorably to assess his moral motives are entirely precluded by the records, and in particular by what the Master said of him! He never hinted at the possibility that Judas may have been just a well-meaning blunderer! What he said was: "One of you is a devil!" "It had been better for him that he had not been born!" And he said it with a sob in His voice!

What a warning flare is this story of one of the Master's men—a flare whose warning none of us dare disregard. If we do, it is at our peril. For unhappily there is nothing very exceptional in a divided heart on the part of those who profess the faith of Christ. Judas only did what many another does—and seems to get away with. For how many give Christ less than the whole of their lives? How many have a love which contests His? In the bright light of reality how many are self-revealed as the slaves of this world, and its tinsel baubles and its deceiving riches? How many are actually robbing the Master whom they acclaim as Judas did?

When one sees what some titular Christians will do for money and its equivalents, how they will sell their good name, how they will lie, how they will deny their loyalties, how they will outrage the honor of the Christian church, how they will pilfer from the bag (not by taking but by withholding), spending more on a single item of self-interest than their total givings to God's work in a year, more on entertainments and self-indulgence, on unnecessary adornment and attire than on the cause of God (so much so, indeed, as to make it impossible for them to give proportionately, not to say adequately, to the work of the gospel), how they will content themselves to be in debt to God for unpaid tithes, a debt they never intend to discharge—for the idea of giving away a "tithe" they deride as absurd quixotism (whereas it isn't even good Judaism, much less Christianity, to give God less!)—when one sees this (and one does see it on every hand) one knows only too unmistakably that some people are flirting with spiritual disaster, as Judas did! That they're trifling with Christ and their own soul! That they're at the old Judas game of trying to make the best of both worlds! The game in which conscience is opposed by expediency, and choices are made between gain and godliness, and destinies are determined. For:

> Still as of old, men by themselves are priced.
> For thirty pieces Judas sold himself—not Christ!

Beware, my friends, of the small beginnings of great tragedies, in which the Master is betrayed into the hands of His enemies, and the betrayer—like Judas, is utterly fooled! Beware of the halfhearted Christian life which can only end in wholehearted and destructive allegiance to the "god of this world"! Beware of the pitiful disaster of honoring the Master with your lips while your heart is actually given to another!

Of course the question will be asked: "Why did the Master ever choose such a man as Judas?" Until a yet more searching question simply clamors for answer: "Why did He choose me?" And the answer is, in both cases, the same—not for what he was! Certainly not for what he became! But for what he might have become! And the resolute prayer voices itself that the Master's verdict may never be "it had been good for that man if he had not been born"; but rather "it has been good for the world that he was born out of due time." For out of him, into its desert wastes, rivers of redemptive influence have flowed. And men call Me "Master" because they knew him as My man!

The Betrayal

Charles Haddon Spurgeon (1834–1892) was undoubtedly the most famous minister of the last century. Converted in 1850, he united with the Baptists and soon began to preach in various places. He became pastor of the Baptist church in Waterbeach in 1851, and three years later he was called to the decaying Park Street Church, London. Within a short time the work began to prosper, a new church was built and dedicated in 1861, and Spurgeon became London's most popular preacher. In 1855, he began to publish his sermons weekly; today they make up the fifty-seven volumes of *The Metropolitan Tabernacle Pulpit*. He founded a pastor's college and several orphanages.

This sermon is taken from *The Metropolitan Tabernacle Pulpit*, Volume 9.

Charles Haddon Spurgeon

6

THE BETRAYAL

And while he yet spake, behold a multitude, and he that was called Judas, one of the twelve, went before them, and drew near unto Jesus to kiss him. But Jesus said unto him, Judas, betrayest thou the Son of man with a kiss? (Luke 22:47–48).

WHEN SATAN HAD BEEN entirely worsted in his conflict with Christ in the garden, the man-devil Judas came upon the scene. As the Parthian in his flight turns around to shoot the fatal arrow, so the arch-enemy aimed another shaft at the Redeemer by employing the traitor into whom he had entered. Judas became the devil's deputy, and a most trusty and serviceable tool he was. The Evil One had taken entire possession of the apostate's heart, and, like the swine possessed of devils, he ran violently downward toward destruction. Well had infernal malice selected the Savior's trusted friend to be his treacherous betrayer, for thus he stabbed at the very center of his broken and bleeding heart.

But, beloved, as in all things God is wiser than Satan, and the Lord of goodness outwits the Prince of Evil, so, in this dastardly betrayal of Christ, prophecy was fulfilled, and Christ was the more surely declared to be the promised Messiah. Was not Joseph a type? and, lo! like that envied youth, Jesus was sold by His own brethren. Was He not to be another Samson, by whose strength the gates of hell should be torn from their posts? lo! like Samson, He is bound by His countrymen and delivered to the adversary. Do you not know that He was the antitype of David? And was not David deserted by Ahithophel, his own familiar friend and counselor? No, brethren, do not the words of the Psalmist receive a literal fulfillment in our Master's betrayal? What prophecy can be more

73

exactly true than the language of Psalms 41 and 55? In the first we read, "Yea, mine own familiar friend, in whom I trusted, which did eat of my bread, hath lifted up his heel against me;" and in 55 the psalmist is yet more clear, "For it was not an enemy that reproached me; then I could have borne it: neither was it he that hated me that did magnify himself against me; then I would have hid myself from him: but it was thou, a man mine equal, my guide, and mine acquaintance. We took sweet counsel together, and walked unto the house of God in company. He hath put forth his hands against such as be at peace with him: he hath broken his covenant. The words of his mouth were smoother than butter, but war was in his heart: his words were softer than oil, yet were they drawn swords."

Even an obscure passage in one of the lesser prophets, must have a literal fulfillment, and for thirty pieces of silver, the price of a base slave, must the Savior be betrayed by His choice friend. Ah! you foul fiend, you shall find at the last that your wisdom is but intensified folly; as for the deep plots and plans of your craft, the Lord shall laugh them to scorn; after all, you are but the unconscious drudge of Him whom you abhor; in all the black work you do so greedily, you are no better than a mean scullion in the royal kitchen of the King of kings.

Without further preface, let us advance to the subject of our Lord's betrayal. First, concentrate your thoughts upon *Jesus, the betrayed one*; and when you have lingered awhile there, solemnly gaze into the villainous countenance of *Judas, the betrayer*—he may prove a beacon to warn us against the sin which genders apostasy.

Jesus, the Betrayed

It is appointed that He must die, but how shall He fall into the hands of His adversaries? Shall they capture Him in conflict? It must not be, lest He appear an unwilling victim. Shall He flee before His foes until He can hide no longer? It is not meet that a sacrifice should be hunted to death. Shall He offer Himself to the foe? That were to excuse His murderers, or be a party to their crime. Shall He be taken accidentally or unawares? That would withdraw from His cup the necessary bitterness which made it wormwood mingled with gall. No, He must be betrayed by His friend that He may bear the utmost depths of suffering, and that in every separate circumstance there may be a well of grief.

One reason for the appointment of the betrayal lay in the fact *that it was ordained that man's sin should reach its culminating point in His death.* God, the great owner of the vineyard, had sent many servants, and the husbandmen had stoned one and cast out another; last of all, He said, "I will send my Son; surely they will reverence my Son." When they slew the heir to win the inheritance, their rebellion had reached its height. The murder of our blessed Lord was the extreme of human guilt; it developed the deadly hatred against God which lurks in the heart of man. When man became a deicide, sin had reached its fullness; and in the black deed of the man by whom the Lord was betrayed, that fullness was all displayed.

If it had not been for a Judas, we had not known how black, how foul, human nature may become. I scorn the men who try to apologize for the treachery of this devil in human form, this son of perdition, this foul apostate. I should think myself a villain if I tried to screen him, and I shudder for the men who dare extenuate his crimes. My brethren, we should feel a deep detestation of this master of infamy; he has gone to his own place, and the anathema of David, part of which was quoted by Peter, has come upon him, "When he shall be judged, let him be condemned: and let his prayer become sin. Let his days be few; and let another take his office." Surely, as the devil was allowed unusually to torment the bodies of men, even so was he let loose to get possession of Judas as he has seldom gained possession of any other man that we might see how foul, how desperately evil is the human heart. Beyond a doubt, however, the main reason for this was *that Christ might offer a perfect atonement for sin.*

We may usually read the sin in the punishment. Man

betrayed his God. Man had the custody of the royal garden, and should have kept its green avenues sacred for communion with his God; but he betrayed the trust; the sentinel was false; he admitted evil into his own heart and so into the paradise of God. He was false to the good name of the Creator, tolerating the insinuation which he should have repelled with scorn. Therefore must Jesus find man a traitor to Him. There must be the counterpart of the sin in the suffering which He endured.

You and I have often betrayed Christ. We have, when tempted, chosen the evil and forsaken the good; we have taken the bribes of hell and have not followed closely with Jesus. It seemed most fitting, then, that He who bore the chastisement of sin should be reminded of its ingratitude and treachery by the things which He suffered.

Besides, brethren, that *cup must be bitter to the last degree which is to be the equivalent for the wrath of God.* There must be nothing consolatory in it; pains must be taken to pour into it all that even divine wisdom can invent of awful and unheard of woe, and this one point— "He that eateth bread with me hath lifted up his heel against me"— was absolutely necessary to intensify the bitterness. Moreover, we feel persuaded that by thus suffering at the hand of a traitor *the Lord became a faithful High Priest,* able to sympathize with us when we fall under the like affliction. Since slander and ingratitude are common calamities, we can come to Jesus with full assurance of faith; He knows these sore temptations for He has felt them in their very worst degree. We may cast every care, and every sorrow upon Him for He cares for us, having suffered with us. Thus, then, in our Lord's betrayal, Scripture was fulfilled, sin was developed, atonement was completed, and the great all-suffering High Priest became able to sympathize with us in every point.

Now let us *look at the treason itself.* You perceive how black it was. Judas was *Christ's servant;* what if I call him His confidential servant. He was a partaker in apostolic ministry and the honor of miraculous gifts. He had been most kindly and indulgently treated. He was a sharer in all the goods of his Master, in fact he fared far better than his Lord, for the Man of Sorrows always took the lion's share of all the pains of poverty and the reproach of slander. He had food and raiment given him out of the common stock, and the Master seems to have indulged him very greatly. The old tradition is that next to the apostle Peter he was the one with whom the Savior most commonly associated. We think there must be a mistake there, for surely John was the Savior's greatest friend; but Judas, as a servant had been treated with the utmost confidence.

You know, brethren, how sore is that blow which comes from a servant in whom we have put unlimited trust. But Judas was more than this: *he was a friend, a trusted friend*. That little bag into which generous women cast their small contributions had been put into his hands, and very wisely too, for he had the financial vein. His main virtue was economy, a very needful quality in a treasurer. As exercising a prudent foresight for the little company and watching the expenses carefully, he was, as far as men could judge, the right man in the right place. He had been thoroughly trusted. I read not that there was an annual audit of his accounts; I do not discover that the Master took him to task as to the expenditure of his privy purse. Everything was given to him, and he gave, at the Master's direction, to the poor, but no account was asked.

This is vile indeed, to be chosen to such a position, to be installed purse-bearer to the King of kings, Chancellor of God's exchequer, and then to turn aside and sell the Savior; this is treason in its uttermost degree. Remember that the world looked upon Judas *as colleague* and partner with our Lord. To a great extent the name of Judas was associated with that of Christ. When Peter, James, or John had done anything amiss, reproachful tongues threw it all on their Master. The Twelve were part and parcel of Jesus of Nazareth. One old commentator says of Judas—"He was Christ's alter ego"—to the people at large there was an identification of each apostle with the leader of the band. And oh! when such associations have been established, and then there is treachery, it is as though our arm should commit treason against our head, or as if our foot should desert the body. This was a stab indeed!

Perhaps, dear brethren, our Lord saw in the person of Judas *a representative man*, the portraiture of the many thousands who in after ages imitated his crime. Did Jesus see in Iscariot all the Judases who betray truth, virtue, and the cross? Did He perceive the multitudes of whom we may say that they were, spiritually, in the loins of Judas? Hymeneus, Alexander, Hermogenes, Philetus, Demas, and others of that tribe, were all before him as he saw the man, his equal, his acquaintance, bartering him away for thirty pieces of silver.

Dear friends, the position of Judas must have tended greatly to aggravate his treason. Even the heathens have taught us that ingratitude is the worst of vices. When Caesar was stabbed by his friend Brutus, the world's poet writes—

> This was the most unkindest cut of all;
> For when the noble Caesar saw him stab,
> Ingratitude, more strong than traitor's arms,
> Quite vanquish'd him; then burst his mighty heart;
> And, in his mantle muffling up his face,
> Even at the base of Pompey's statua, great Caesar fell.

Many ancient stories, both Greek and Roman, we might quote to show the abhorrence which the heathens entertain toward ingratitude and treachery. Certain, also, of their own poets, such, for instance, as Sophocles, have poured out burning words upon deceitful friends; but we have no time to prove what you will all admit, that nothing can be more cruel, nothing more full of anguish, than to be sold to destruction by one's bosom friend. The closer the foeman comes the deeper will be the stab he gives; if we admit him to our heart, and give him our closest intimacy, then can he wound us in the most vital part.

Let us notice, dear friends, while we look at the breaking heart of our agonizing Savior, the manner in which He met this affliction. He had been much in prayer; prayer had overcome His dreadful agitation; He was very calm; and we need to be very calm when we are forsaken by a friend. Observe His gentleness. The first word He spoke to Judas, when the traitor had polluted his cheek with a kiss, was this—"FRIEND!" FRIEND!! Note that! Not "Thou hateful miscreant," but "Friend, wherefore art thou come?" not "Wretch, wherefore dost thou dare to stain my cheek with thy foul and lying lips?" no, "Friend, wherefore art thou come?" Ah! if there had been anything good left in Judas, this would have brought it out. If he had not been an unmitigated, incorrigible, thrice-dyed traitor, his avarice must have lost its power at that instant, and he would have cried—"My master! I came to betray You, but that generous word has won my soul; here, if You must be bound, I will be bound with You; I make a full confession of my infamy!"

Our Lord added these words—there is reproof in them, but notice how kind they are still, how much too good for such a caitiff—"Judas, betrayest thou the Son of Man with a kiss?" I can conceive that the tears gushed from His eyes, and that His voice faltered, when He thus addressed His own familiar friend and acquaintance— "Betrayest *thou*," My Judas, My treasurer, "betrayest thou *the Son of Man*," your suffering, sorrowing Friend, whom you have seen naked and poor, and without a place whereon to lay His head. Betray you *the Son of Man*—and do you prostitute the fondest of all endearing signs—*a kiss*—that which should be a symbol of loyalty to the King, shall it be the badge of your treachery—that which was reserved for affection as her best symbol—do you make it the instrument of My destruction? Betray you the Son of Man with a kiss?

Oh! if he had not been given up to hardness of heart, if the Holy Spirit had not utterly left him, surely this son of perdition would have fallen prostrate yet again, and weeping out his very soul, would have cried—"No, I cannot betray You, You suffering Son of man; forgive, forgive; spare Yourself; escape from this bloodthirsty crew, and pardon Your treacherous disciple!" But no, no word of compunction while the silver is at stake! Afterward came the sorrow that works death, which drove him, like Ahithophel, his prototype, to court the gallows to escape remorse. This, also, must have aggravated the woe of our beloved Lord, when He saw the final impenitence of the traitor, and read the tearful doom of that man of whom He had once said, "it would be better for him that he had never been born."

Beloved, I would have you fix your eyes on your Lord in your quiet meditations as being thus despised and rejected of men, a man of sorrows and acquainted with grief; and gird up the loins of your minds, counting it no strange thing if this fiery trial should come upon you, but being determined that though your Lord should be betrayed by His most eminent disciples, yet, through His grace you will cling to Him in shame and in suffering, and will follow Him, if needs be, even to death. God give us grace to see the vision of His nailed hands and feet, and remembering that all this came from the treachery of a friend, let us be very jealous of ourselves, lest we crucify the Lord afresh and put Him to an open shame by betraying Him in our conduct, or in our words, or in our thoughts.

Judas, the Betrayer

Grant me your attention while we make an estimate of the man by whom the Son of man was betrayed. I would call your attention, dear friends, *to his position and public character*. Judas was *a preacher*; no, he was a foremost preacher, "he obtained part of this ministry," said the apostle Peter. He was not simply one of the seventy; he had been selected by the Lord Himself as one of the Twelve, an honorable member of the college of the apostles. Doubtless he had preached the gospel so that many had been gladdened by his voice, and miraculous powers had been vouchsafed to him, so that at his word the sick had been healed, deaf ears had been opened, and the blind had been made to see; no, there is no doubt that he who could not keep the devil out of himself, had cast devils out of others.

Yet how are you fallen from heaven, O Lucifer, son of the morning! He that was as a prophet in the midst of the people, and spoke with the tongue of the learned, whose word and wonders proved that he had been with Jesus and had learned of Him—he betrays his Master. Understand, my brethren, that no gifts can ensure grace, and that no position of honor or usefulness in the church will necessarily prove our being true to our Lord and Master. Doubtless there are bishops in hell, and crowds of those who once occupied the pulpit are now condemned forever to bewail their hypocrisy. You that are church officers do not conclude that because you enjoy the confidence of the church that therefore of an absolute certainty the grace of God is in you. Perhaps it is the most dangerous of all positions for a man to become well known and much respected by the religious world, and yet to be rotten at the core. To be where others can observe our faults is a healthy thing though painful; but to live with beloved friends who would not believe it possible for us to do wrong, and who if they saw us err would make excuses for us—this is to be where it is next to impossible for us ever to be aroused if our hearts be not right with God. To have a fair reputation and a false heart is to stand upon the brink of hell.

Judas *took a very high degree officially.* He had the distinguished honor of being entrusted with the Master's financial concerns, and this, after all, was no small degree to which to attain. The Lord, who knows how to use all sorts of gifts, perceived what gift the man had. He knew that Peter's unthinking impetuosity would soon empty the bag and leave the company in great straits, and if he had entrusted it to John, his loving spirit might have been cajoled into unwise benevolence toward beggars of unctuous tongue; he might even have spent the little moneys in buying alabaster boxes whose precious ointments should anoint the Master's head. He gave the bag to Judas, and it was discreetly, prudently, and properly used; there is no doubt he was the most judicious person, and fitted to occupy the post.

But oh! dear friends, if the Master shall choose any of us who are ministers or church officers, and give us a very distinguished position; if our place in the ranks shall be that of commanding officers, so that even our brother ministers look up to us with esteem, and our fellow elders or deacons regard us as being fathers in Israel—oh! if we turn, if we prove false, how damnable shall be our end at the last! What a blow shall we give to the heart of the church, and what derision will be made in hell!

You will observe that the character of Judas *was openly an admirable one.* I find not that he committed himself in any way. Not the slightest speck defiled his moral character so far as others could perceive. He was no boaster, like Peter; he was free enough from the rashness which cries, "Though all men should forsake thee yet will not I." He asks no place on the right hand of the throne, his ambition is of another sort. He does not ask idle questions. The Judas who asks questions is "not Iscariot." Thomas and Philip are often prying into deep matters, but not Judas. He receives truth as it is taught him, and when others are offended and walk no more with Jesus, he faithfully adheres to Him, having golden reasons for so doing. He does not indulge in the lusts of the flesh or in the pride of life. None of the disciples suspected him of hypocrisy; they said at the table, "Lord, is it I?" They never said, "Lord, is it Judas?"

It was true he had been filching for months, but then he did it by littles, and covered his defalcations so well by financial manipulations that he ran no risk of detection from the honest unsuspecting fishermen with whom he associated. Like some merchants and traders we have heard of—invaluable gentlemen as chairmen of speculating companies and general managers of swindling banks—he could abstract a decent percentage and yet make the accounts exactly tally. The gentlemen who have learned of Judas, manage to cook the accounts most admirably for the shareholders, so as to get a rich joint for their own table; over which they, no doubt, entreat the divine blessing.

Judas was, in his known life, a most admirable person. He would have been an alderman ere long there is no doubt, and being very pious and richly-gifted, his advent at churches or chapels would have created intense satisfaction. "What a discreet and influential person," say the deacons. "Yes," replies the minister, "what an acquisition to our councils; if we could elect him to office he would be of eminent service to the church." I believe that the Master chose him as apostle on purpose that we might not be at all surprised if we find such a man a minister in the pulpit, or a colleague of the minister, working as an officer in Christ's church. These are solemn things, my brethren; let us take them to heart, and if any of us wear a good character among men and stand high in office, let this question come home close to us—"Lord, is it I? Lord, is it I?" Perhaps he who shall last ask the question is just the man who ought to have asked it first.

But, secondly, I call your attention *to his real nature and sin.* Judas was a man with a conscience. He could not afford to do without it. He was no Sadducee who could fling religion overboard; he had strong religious tendencies. He was no debauched person; he never spent a two-pence in vice on his life, not that he loved vice less, but that he loved the two-pence more. Occasionally he was generous, but then it was with other people's money. Well did he watch his lovely charge, the bag.

He had a conscience, I say, and a ferocious conscience it was when it once broke the chain, for it was his conscience which made him hang himself. But then it was a conscience that did not sit regularly on the throne; it reigned by fits and starts. Conscience was not the leading element. Avarice predominated over conscience. He would get money, if honestly, he liked that best, but if he could not get it conscientiously, then anyhow in the world. He was but a small trader; his gains were no great things, or else he would not have sold Christ for so small a sum as that—ten pounds at the outside, of our money at its present value—some three or four pounds, as it was in those days. It was a poor price to take for the Master; but then a little money was a great thing to him. He had been poor; he had joined Christ with the idea that he would soon be proclaimed King of the Jews, and that then he should become a nobleman and be rich. Finding Christ a long while in coming to His kingdom, he had taken little by little, enough to lay by in store; and now, fearing that he was to be disappointed in all his dreams, and never having had any care for Christ, but only for himself, he gets out of what he thinks to have been a gross mistake in the best way he can, and makes money by his treason against his Lord.

Brethren, I do solemnly believe that of all hypocrites, those are the persons of whom there is the least hope whose God is their money. You may reclaim a drunkard; thank God, we have seen many instances of that; and even a fallen Christian who has given way to vice may loathe his lust and return from it; but I fear me that the cases in which a man who is cankered with covetousness has ever been saved are so few, that they might be written on your fingernail.

This is a sin which the world does not rebuke; the most faithful minister can scarce smit its forehead. God knows what thunders I have launched out against men who are all for this world, and yet pretend to be Christ's followers; but yet they always say, "It is not for me." What I should call stark naked covetousness, they call prudence, discretion, economy, and so on; and actions which I would scorn to spit upon, they will do, and think their hands quite clean after they have done them, and still sit as God's people sit, and hear as God's people hear, and think that after they have sold Christ for paltry gain, they will go to heaven.

O souls, souls, souls, beware, beware, beware, most of all of greed! It is not money, nor the lack of money, but the love of money which is the root of all evil. It is not getting it; it is not even keeping it; it is loving it; it is making it your god; it is looking at that as the main chance, and not considering the cause of Christ, nor the truth of Christ, nor the holy life of Christ, but being ready to sacrifice everything for gains' sake. Oh! such men make giants in sin; they shall be set up forever as butts for infernal laughter; their damnation shall be sure and just.

The third point is *the warning which Judas received and the way in which he persevered.* Just think—the night before he sold his Master what do you think the Master did? Why, He washed his feet! And yet he sold Him! Such condescension! Such love! Such familiarity! He took a towel, and girded Himself, and washed Judas' feet! And yet those very feet brought Judas as a guide to them that took Jesus! And you remember what He said when He had washed his feet. "Now ye are clean, but not all;" and he turned a tearful eye on Judas. What a warning for him! What could be more explicit?

Then when the Supper came, and they began to eat and drink together, the Lord said—"One of you shall betray me." That was plain enough; and a little farther on He said explicitly—"He that dippeth with me in the dish the same is he." What opportunities for repentance! He cannot say he had not a faithful preacher. What could have been more personal? If he does not repent now, what is to be done?

Moreover, Judas saw that which was enough to make a heart of adamant bleed; he saw Christ with agony on His face, for it was just after Christ had said, "Now is my soul troubled," that Judas left the feast and went out to sell his Master. That face, so full of grief, ought to have turned him, must have turned him, if he had not been given up and left alone to deliver over his soul unto his own devices. What language could have been more thundering than the words of Jesus Christ when He said, "Woe unto that man by whom the Son of man is betrayed; it had been good for that man if he had not been born." He had said, "Have not I chosen you twelve, and one of you is a devil."

Now, if while these thunders rolled over his head, and the lightning flashes pointed at his person, if, then, this man was not aroused, what a hell of infernal pertinacity and guilt must have been within his soul! Oh! but if any of you, if any of you shall sell Christ for the sake of keeping the shop open on Sunday, if you shall sell Christ for the extra wages you may earn for falsehood—oh! if you shall sell Christ for the sake of the hundred pounds that you may lay hold of by a villainous contract—if you do that, you do not perish unwarned. I come into this pulpit to please no man among you. God knows if I knew more of your follies you should have them pointed out yet more plainly; if I knew more of the tricks of business, I would not flinch to speak of them! But, O sirs, I do conjure you by the blood of Judas, who hanged himself at last, turn you—if such there be—turn you from this evil, if haply your sin may be blotted out!

Let us for one minute *notice the act itself.* He sought out his own temptation. He did not wait for the devil to come to him; he went after the devil. He went to the chief priests and said, "What will ye give me?" One of the old Puritan divines says, "This is not the way people generally trade; they tell their own price." Judas says, "What will you give me? Anything you like. The Lord of life and glory sold at the buyer's own price. What will you give me?" And another very prettily puts it, "What could they give him? What did the man want? He did not want food and raiment; he fared as well as his Master and the other disciples; he had enough; he had all that his needs could crave, and yet he said, What will you give me? What will you give me? What will you give me?"

Alas! some people's religion is grounded on that one question—"What will you give me?" Yes, they would go to church if there are any charities given away there, but if there were more to be got by not going they would do that. "What will you give me?" Some of these people are not even so wise as Judas. Ah! there is a man over yonder who would sell the Lord for a crown, much more for ten pounds, as Judas did! Why, there are some who will sell Christ for the smallest piece of silver in our currency. They are tempted to deny their Lord, tempted to act in an unhallowed way, though the gains are so paltry that a year's worth of them would not come to much.

No subject could be more dreadful than this if we really would but look at it carefully. This temptation happens to each of us. Do not deny it. We all like to gain; it is but natural that we should; the propensity to acquire is in every mind, and under lawful restrictions it is not an improper propensity; but when it comes into conflict with our allegiance to our Master, and in a world like this it often will, we must overcome it or perish. There will arise occasions with some of you many times in a week in which it is God—or gain, "Christ, or the thirty pieces of silver," and therefore I am the more urgent in pressing this on you. Do not, though the world should bid its highest, though it should heap its comforts upon one another, and add fame, and honor, and respect, do not, I pray you, forsake your Master.

There have been such cases; cases of persons who used to come here, but they found they did not get on, because Sunday was the best day's trade in the week; they had some good feelings, some good impressions once, but they have lost them now. We have known others who have said, "Well, you see, I did once think I loved the Lord, but my business went so badly when I came up to the house of God that I left it; I renounced my profession."

Ah, Judas! ah, Judas! ah, Judas! let me call you by your name, for such you are! This is the sin of the apostate over again; God help you to repent of it, and go, not to any priest, but to Christ and make confession, if haply you may be saved.

You perceive that in the act of selling Christ, Judas was faithful to his master. "Faithful to his master?" you say. Yes, his master was the devil, and having made an agreement with him he carried it out honestly. Some people are always very honest with the devil. If they say they will do a wrong thing they say they ought to do it because *they said* they would; as if any oath could be binding on a man if it be an oath to do wrong? "I will never go into that house again," some have said, and they have said afterward, "Well, I wish I had not said it." Was it a wrong thing? What is your oath then? It was an oath given to the devil. What was that foolish promise but a promise to Satan, and will you be faithful to him? Ah! would God that you were faithful to Christ! Would that any of us were as true to Christ as Satan's servants are to their master!

Judas betrayed his Master with a kiss. That is how most apostates do it; it is always with a kiss. Did you ever read an infidel book in your life which did not begin with profound respect for truth? I never have. Even modern ones, when bishops write them, always begin like that.

They betray the Son of man with a kiss. Did you ever read a book of bitter controversy which did not begin with such a sickly lot of humility, such sugar, such butter, such treacle, such everything sweet and soft, that you said, "Ah! there is sure to be something bad here, for when people begin so softly and sweetly, so humbly and so smoothly, depend upon it they have rank hatred in their hearts." The most devout looking people are often the most hypocritical in the world.

We conclude with the repentance of Judas. He did repent; he did repent; but it was the repentance that works death. He did make a confession, but there was no respect to the deed itself, but only to its consequences. He was very sorry that Christ was condemned. Some latent love that he had once had to a kind Master came up when he saw that he was condemned. He did not think, perhaps, it would come to that; he may have had a hope that he would escape out of their hands, and then he would keep his thirty pieces of silver, and perhaps sell him over again. Perhaps he thought that he would rid himself from their hands by some miraculous display of power, or would proclaim the kingdom, and so he himself would only be hastening on that very blessed consummation.

Friends, the man who repents of consequences does not repent. The ruffian repents of the gallows but not of the murder, and that is no repentance at all. Human law, of course, must measure sin by consequences, but God's law does not. There is a pointsman on a railway who neglects his duty; there is a collision on the line, and people are killed; well, it is manslaughter to this man through his carelessness. But that pointsman, perhaps, many times before had neglected his duty, but no accident came of it, and then he walked home and said, "Well, I have done no wrong." Now the wrong, mark you, is never to be measured by the accident, but by the thing itself, and if you have committed an offense and you have escaped undetected it is just as vile in God's eye; if you have done wrong and Providence has prevented the natural result of the wrong, the honor of that is with God, but you are as guilty as if your sin had been carried out to its fullest consequences, and the whole world set ablaze. Never measure sin by consequences, but repent of them as they are in themselves.

Though being sorry for consequences, since these are unalterable, this man was led to remorse. He sought a tree, adjusted the rope, and hanged himself, but in his haste he hanged himself so badly that the rope broke, he fell over a precipice, and there we read his bowels gushed out; he lay a mangled mass at the bottom of the cliff, the horror of every one who passed.

Now you that make a gain of godliness—if there be such here—you may not come to a suicide's end, but take the lesson home. Mr. Keach, my venerable predecessor, gives at the end of one of his volumes of sermons, the death of a Mr. John Child. John Child had been a Dissenting minister, and for the sake of gain, to get a living, he joined the Episcopalians against his conscience; he sprinkled infants, and practiced all the other paraphernalia of the church against his conscience. At last, at last, he was arrested with such terrors for having done what he had, that he renounced his living, took to a sick bed, and his dying oaths, and blasphemies, and curses, were something so dreadful, that his case was the wonder of that age. Mr. Keach wrote a full account of it, and many went to try what they could do to comfort the man, but he would say, "Get ye hence; get ye hence; it is of no use; I have sold Christ."

You know, also, the wonderful death of Francis Spira. In all literature, there is nothing so awful as the death of Spira. The man had known the truth; he stood well among reformers; he was an honored and, to a certain extent, apparently a faithful man; but he went back to the church of Rome; he apostatized; and then when conscience was aroused he did not fly to Christ, but he looked at the consequences instead of at the sin, and so, feeling that the consequences could not be altered, he forgot that the sin might be pardoned, and perished in agonies extreme.

May it never be the unhappy lot of any of us to stand by such a deathbed; but the Lord have mercy upon us now, and make us search our hearts. Those of you who say, "We do not want that sermon," are probably the persons who need it most. He who shall say, "Well, we have no Judas amongst us," is probably a Judas himself. Oh! search yourselves; turn out every cranny; look in every corner of your soul, to see whether your religion be for Christ's sake, and for truth's sake, and for God's sake, or whether it be a profession which you take up because it is a respectable thing, a profession which you keep up because it keeps you up. The Lord search us and try us, and bring us to know our ways.

And now, in conclusion—there is a Savior, and that Savior is willing to receive us now. If I am not a saint, yet I am a sinner. Would it not be best for all of us to go again to the fountain, and wash and be clean. Let each of us go anew, and say, "Master, You know what I am; I know not myself; but, if I be wrong, make me right; if I be right, keep me so. My trust is in You. Keep me now, for Your own sake, Jesus." Amen.

More Than Remorse—Real Repentance!

Walter A. Maier (1893–1950) was known around the world as the speaker on "The Lutheran Hour," heard over more than a thousand radio stations. Many of his faithful listeners did not realize that this effective communicator was also professor of Old Testament and Semitic Languages at Concordia Seminary in St. Louis. It was said the Maier spent one hour in preparation for each minute that he spoke on the radio. Many of his radio sermons were published in volumes still treasured by those who appreciate good preaching.

This sermon is found in *Courage in Christ*, published by Concordia Publishing House, St. Louis, in 1941.

Walter A. Maier

7

MORE THAN REMORSE— REAL REPENTANCE!

> Judas, which had betrayed him, when he saw that he was condemned, repented himself and brought again the thirty pieces of silver to the chief priests and elders, saying, I have sinned in that I have betrayed the innocent blood. And they said, What is that to us? See thou to that. And he cast down the pieces of silver in the Temple and departed and went and hanged himself (Matthew 27:3–5).

SORROW FOR OUR SINS, remorse over our failures, can become life's most terrifying scourge. Every day your letters testify to the fury of an aroused conscience. A Kentucky young woman writes that since she violated her chastity, only to be jilted, she can hardly find forgetfulness even in sleep. An Indiana couple, each previously divorced and now married to each other against the Scriptures, is tortured by the realization that for years both have openly lived in adultery. A county official in a Western State who stole public money and lost it in speculation is almost paralyzed by fear over the State auditor's impending visit. A Michigan girl, because of previous transgressions, is haunted by the terror of having committed the unpardonable sin. A Kansas listener laments that she has been robbed of peace because she opposed her parents, neglected them in their needs, and, now they are dead, can never make amends. Although forty years have elapsed since the crime, an Ohio mother is relentlessly pursued by remorse for having destroyed her unborn child.

Life is not secure under the torment of self-condemnation. The appalling suicide toll in the United States takes many who mistakenly felt themselves driven to self-destruction under the lash of an outraged conscience. We are, of course, accustomed to read of suicides after naval disasters when a captain (by a code of the sea which all civilized nations should revoke) deliberately goes down with his ship. For years self-murder has been an accepted social escape in Japan. There military officers who fail are expected to destroy themselves by the prescribed rites of *hara-kiri*. Annually hundreds of Nipponese young people, frustrated in love, join hands, leap into the crater of a favorite volcano, and are burned to cinders by molten lava. How shocking to hear that the number of suicides in the United States is practically as large as in non-Christ-ian Japan!

The most intense sorrow over missteps and mistakes is not enough. A lifetime of regrets is not sufficient. Suicide only brings eternal horror and suffering. We must learn the lesson millions in America have forgotten, the truth which can change our existence from years of extended fears to a career of sustained peace in Christ, the convic-tion that for the removal of our sins we must, beholding Jesus, have

More Than Remorse—Real Repentance!

To this end may God's Holy Spirit guide us in our study of the warning and, by contrast, the comfort offered by Matthew 27:3–5: "Judas, which had betrayed him, when he saw that he was condemned, repented himself and brought again the thirty pieces of silver to the chief priests and elders, saying, I have sinned in that I have betrayed the innocent blood. And they said, What is that to us? See thou to that. And he cast down the pieces of silver in the Temple and departed and went and hanged himself" (Matt. 27:3–5).

Remorse Is Not Enough

We often think of Judas as a hideous monster, an ugly, misshapen, beastlike creature, a veritable Frankenstein, while in truth he was an ordinary man, doubtless with many amiable qualities. When as a boy he played in the streets and fields of Kerioth, a little village in the South, often, doubtless, his parents, smiling at their happy child, dreamed of the day when their Judas would be a re-spected, successful citizen, an elder in the community council, even as you fathers and mothers like to envision your sons as making their mark in the world. After he grew to manhood, he cannot have been destitute of ideals, for a day of destiny came when a Stranger, mysterious, yet compelling, a Galilean Teacher called Jesus of Nazareth, preached a heart-searching message and confronted Judas with the invitation, *"Follow Me!"* Although he knew that obedience to the Lord meant bearing the cross of affliction, Judas gave up everything to accept the Savior's leadership.

Among the Twelve he, the only disciple from Judea, gained a certain distinction; for before long he was entrusted with the treasury, meager though it was. We search in vain throughout the early gospel records for evidence of his disloyalty; there is none. Like his eleven comrades he, too, acclaimed Christ, who he thought would liberate Israel and establish a magnificent kingdom. When, after a hard sermon by Jesus, many of His followers forsook Him, Judas did not leave.

I am trying to impress on you the truth that Judas was one of us. If in a surge of self-righteousness some of you protest, "Well, I certainly would never do what he did!" you don't know Judas, and you don't know yourself! The only people who cannot commit his sin are the heathen who have never heard of Jesus; those are the closest to repeating his betrayal who, as he, are nearest Christ. *"Let him that thinketh he standeth take heed lest he fall,"* the eternal Word warns; and not until we see in that thankless disciple the same guilty, evil impulses which occupy our own hearts are we honestly concerned with our immortal souls' welfare.

The trouble started with Judas where it often begins in our lives: with money. Other explanations, of course, have been advanced. A favorite theory claims that Judas wanted to bring Christ's cause to a climax; so he betrayed his Lord only to create a situation by which Jesus would be obliged to demonstrate His power. But the Scriptures know nothing of this. The gospels tell us that Judas loved gold; and gradually, it seems, he became disappointed in Christ. His materialistic imagination had pictured the Savior with a resplendent crown on His head; but these hopes were soon replaced by resentment when our Lord spoke of submission to His enemies, of martyrdom and a death of shame. It may well be that Judas argued within himself: "I will still get something from following Christ! The Temple authorities want to put Him out of the way! They can use me, and I will make them pay."

Whatever his reasoning was, he went to the priests, perhaps soothing his conscience with the alibi that these men were supposed to be representatives of the Most High, that they would welcome his betrayal as a pious, God-pleasing act. People use the same tactics today. Sin loses its stigma if the church can be made to approve it. The unjustly divorced often want a preacher to solemnize their second matrimonial venture. The bereaved relatives of a foul-mouthed infidel who died without a thought of Jesus are eager for a Christian burial, since it would remove the disgrace. Gamblers like to have roulette wheels, dice, cards, games of chance, in congregational buildings for the sanction and prestige that religion offers. War-promoters—and we shall constantly hear more of them—piously call the present hostilities a battle for God, a crusade for Christianity, a struggle for the faith, so that the churches' influence may be enlisted to throw our youth into the vortex of Europe's war.

But we need much more than outward religious sanction to justify our actions. It must be said to the shame of certain church groups that frequently they have become part and party to proposals which utterly repudiate Christ. In the blessed name of Him who is Peace and Love clerics have preached hatred and destruction. They have sanctioned murder, theft, false witness, divorce, adultery, unjust, aggressive wars of conquest.

Masking his hypocrisy in mock piety, Judas approached the religious leaders with the age-old question of grasping greed, *"What will ye give me?"* And those Temple officials, the men required to show God's holiness, bargained with a traitor! "Abhorrent!" you exclaim, but not so depraved, I answer, that a similar desire to get rid of Jesus does not animate some churchmen today. They exhibit the same outward zeal of Annas, Caiaphas, the scribes, and the Pharisees, but they also have the same hatred for the biblical Christ. *"Away with Him!"* their cry reechoes, repeating the malicious verdict of the first Good Friday. "Away with Jesus as God's Son and the world's Savior, the virgin-born, crucified, resurrected, ascended Redeemer! Away with Him as the only Hope of a perishing world!" This rejection has become so widespread and influential that it can keep gospel broadcasts off the country's largest stations. Voices regarded as authoritatively Protestant often reject the basic, biblical truths. If you love Christ, work and pray that this discarding of His deathless Word be stopped in many churches now!

"What will ye give me?"—this barter of greed is quite modern. *"The love of money"* is still *"the root of all"* (kinds of) *"evil."* Stripped of its disguises, most war is promoted by avarice. Commercial supremacy, domination of the seas, more territory, fertile farmlands, productive oil-fields, rich mineral deposits, economic ascendancy—these are the objectives for which world meddlers have laid unsuspecting, high-idealed youth on gory altars before the idol of war in a human sacrifice far more despicable than the Canaanite child-offerings in Hinnom's valley. *"What will ye give me?"*—this selfish inquiry motivates the struggle in our American industrial circles, where, instead of cooperative harmony, we witness growing antagonism. *"What will ye give me?"*—this personal profit-seeking urges Christians to stretch out their hands for unholy gain in a hundred different forms of theft, which some of you have been able to conceal, not, however, from your conscience and Almighty God.

Judas' sin was heightened because he was ready to sell a life for blood-money. It has been questioned whether he actually believed the Savior's enemies would go to the extent of crucifixion. But how could anyone accompany Jesus for three years and doubt that the priestly venom would be satisfied with anything less than death? Many today share the same guilt. This generation particularly should read carefully the scandals of past wars with their hideous profiteering. During the first world conflict British soldiers in the Dardanelles were mowed down by British guns in enemy hands. Austrians on the Galician front were killed by rifles originally made or repaired by Austrians. Two French firms were able to import, on their own account, German steel through Switzerland. We, too, have tragic records of spoiled meat, inferior equipment, defective weapons deliberately sold to American armies; and even now a Congressional committee has been appointed to investigate evidences of profiteering in our defense program. Not many forms of depravity are lower than this clutching desire to march on to wealth over bodies sacrificed to greed. Few figures are more despicable than international munitions-manufacturers who, though decorated and knighted by a dozen governments, as some were, grew rich and powerful through unscrupulous arms traffic.

Many of you, however, who would shrink from harming your neighbor in his body may for the sake of profit cause his soul to suffer. With the drop in morality that war brings already unmistakable (London reports an increase of 40 percent in juvenile crime.); with taxi dancehalls springing up around our half-finished military camps (and I pause to ask you Christian young men in the service for loyalty, not only to your country, but also to your Christ); with a growing army of Americans making their livelihood directly or indirectly from the sale of suggestive books and sex magazines, pictures or plays that glorify sin, drugs or drink that injure the body and serve lust, there can be only one course for those who serve Christ, and that is specified by the command *"Come out from among them, and be ye separate!"*

I do not stand before this microphone to utter a blanket condemnation; for the Savior's word is clear, *"Judge not, and ye shall not be judged!"* I do pray, however, that the Spirit may fortify these words: If you work as owner or employee in an office, factory, store, or business where the enterprise deliberately seeks to take people away from Jesus, attacks the Bible, assaults Christian morality, destroys the ideals of truth, purity, and honesty; if young people can point their finger at you, charging, *"You* helped lead me on the road to sin," then remember Judas! Ask our Lord's forgiveness and the strength to stop the heinous wrong, give up that destructive employment forever! This will take courage. Immediately you will hear whispered objections: "Where can I get another job? This position pays a good salary. If I don't make or sell this, someone else will. I give a large check to the church every week." But that comes from the same satanic Tempter who brought Judas to fall. Steadfastly look to Jesus, and as you exalt Him, you will find His promise fulfilled, *"If any man serve me, him will my Father honor."*

Lured by avarice, Judas not only deserted Christ, connived with His enemies, bargained for blood-money; as history's most damnable Fifth Columnist he sold the Savior, not for 30,000,000 pieces of silver nor even 30,000. We could understand how a depraved wretch might have been tempted by such fortunes. But thirty paltry pieces! Hardly enough to buy food and clothing for a few months! Barely sufficient for the priests to purchase an unwanted, out-of-the-way piece of land as a potter's field, the burial place of the unclaimed or criminally dead! Christ sold for thirty pieces of silver, $18 in our money! "How incredible!" we exclaim. Satan does not always have to bid that high. Some of you have sold Christ for less. A wild night's entertainment which cost your companion, say, $15; a $9.98 set of antichristian scientific volumes which an unbeliever *gave* you; a *free* visit to a spiritist medium, who usually charges a dollar; a fifty-cent blasphemous book or a five-cent blue paper-covered infidel pamphlet that some atheist sent you without charge—these may be the only inducements the devil had to offer in turning you against Christ. For trivial honors and the smallest sensual satisfaction people are sometimes ready to adopt Judas's tactics and beneath smirking hypocrisy array themselves against Christ.

The gospel narratives do not tell us how Judas spent the time after he placed the kiss of betrayal on the Savior's cheek. If it is true, as a few scholars claim, that he followed Christ at a distance and witnessed the beginning of His trials, we understand the more clearly why a startling change gradually overtook him. At first perhaps Judas played with the silver pieces, letting them fall through his fingers, polishing them, placing them in rows, jingling them at his ears, dreaming of the power the money-mad think they can conjure with clicking coins. But *"when he saw that"* Jesus *"was condemned,"* the attraction of that minted silver suddenly vanished. The treachery, which had seemed such an easy, cunning scheme, now became an avalanche of terror.

Do you know that Judas, recoiling from his despicable sin, showed more concern than some of you? He at least realized his monstrous crime and hated it; you see only the sensual appeal of your transgression and love it. You—this is your boast—will do what you want, and no one can stop *you!* The Lord Jesus Christ's name is just an aid to your profanity. For your soul's sake I pray God that He will hurl you down from your self-conceited unbelief, if necessary, into the depth of suffering, so that, helpless, you can learn what even Judas knew, "Sin never pays, while the sinner always pays." If some of you young people who once thought that there could be nothing sweeter than the forbidden fruits begin to experience an aftertaste of bitterness, thank God! You will never know Christ until you recognize your own sin!

Judas went a step farther. He returned to the priests, hoping he could secure help in the Temple; yet just as little as people today can find soul-comfort through any religious teacher not blessed by God, so the distracted disciple vainly sought guidance in the Sanctuary. Terrified, he confessed the enormity of his crime, saying, *"I have sinned!"* And then Judas, the hypocrite, the traitor, became the first in the story of the Savior's suffering to declare Jesus not guilty. Hear his cry reecho through the Temple, *"I have betrayed the innocent blood!"* Again, Judas was far in advance of many modern Americans; he confessed his sin, while voices throughout the country in education, literature, philosophy, science, give it new names, excuse it, even justify it, and—this low have they stooped!—even glorify it! Judas told the men who had directed the plot against Christ that Jesus was blameless;

let this statement from the lips of our Lord's archenemy urge you to recognize that Jesus has always been innocent of every calumny and attack perverted men have hurled against Him. Unless you understand that our Lord was guiltless and that the death penalty placed on His stainless body and soul was incurred by your transgression, you cannot know true repentance nor find the pathway to heaven.

The priests coldly shrugged their shoulders as they replied, *"What is that to us? See thou to that!"* and showed the devilish unconcern which always marks sin. Many of you recall how friends who coaxed you into wrongdoing were the first to turn against you. Despite priestly indifference, however, Judas' conscience continued to drive him on. He tried to make restitution. As impossible as it was for him to rescue Christ from His enemies, he could at least rid himself of the blood-profit gained through the suffering of the Innocent One, and in despair he hurled the thirty pieces of silver to the Sanctuary floor.

Have you tried to make restitution for your sins? If you have stolen money, have you returned it? If you live in an illicit relationship, are you ready to stop and do what God expects of you? If people have suffered through your greed, have you done anything to compensate them? The nation has a conscience fund in Washington, and through receipt of smaller sums it has grown to sizable proportions; but if all money and property sinfully acquired could be returned to the government or defrauded individuals, the country's financial problem would be minimized and millions now destitute could live in comfort. It may be too late to make amends, but unless you do everything humanly possible to refund your thefts, you cannot stand before the Almighty!

As the money rolled on the floor, Judas ran from the Temple in headlong flight, the doom of death written on his countenance. Fear such as only the damned can experience pursued him like hellhounds of endless remorse. Completely in Satan's control, he ended eternally damned; for we read, *"He . . . went and hanged himself."* The carefree child that once played in the lanes of Judean Kerioth, the disciple eager to serve Christ, now dangled in a suicide's noose, until either the rope or tree branch broke, and he fell headlong into death and—hell!

Do you say: "What a fool Judas was! People with any degree of intelligence can avoid what he did"? Are you sure? Can you prove the popular theory that education is the best preventive of self-destruction? Why is it that intellectual leaders and university graduates are frequently numbered among those who take their own lives? Unless you are ready to go farther than Judas went, you have absolutely no assurance that your end must be different from his.

Real Repentance Is Necessary

Judas' suicide impresses on us that more than remorse is necessary. We must have real repentance in Christ! None of life's fears is more treacherous and destructive than the gnawing despair of an aroused conscience. Richard III of England, who murdered his two innocent nephews, kept an unsheathed sword at his bedside and constantly fought invisible imaginary foes. Charles IX of France, who signed the death warrant for tens of thousands of Protestants mowed down in the Saint Bartholomew massacre, asked for music when he awakened at night to soothe his terrorized soul and take his thoughts from the horror of his sin. No matter how intense your remorse may be, if you stop where Judas did, you can cry your eyes dry every day, count each long hour of the night in sleepless anxiety until you collapse in a nervous breakdown; without Christ this is all wasted energy, futile suffering!

It is not enough to declare, "I am sorry!" Dogs show a sort of creature sorrow when punished for wrong-doing! It is not sufficient to resolve, "I will stop this evil. I promise to make good what I have done wrong!" Educated Greek and Roman pagans said the same thing; yet they ended without the assurance of forgiveness! It is not enough to know who Jesus is, to proclaim His innocence. Even the Mohammedan Koran gives the Savior greater glory without being able to offer its followers the pledge of pardon. The factor which makes repentance acceptable in God's sight is the faith by which we place our entire hope for pardon on the Lord Jesus. Only when repentance is made in His name, but always when contrite hearts are lifted first to His cross and then to the open heavens, can we be sure that our sins are removed.

Beholding our Redeemer on the cross, we are to believe, with hearts freed from every doubt, that *"He was wounded for our transgressions, He was bruised for our iniquities, the chastisement of our peace was upon Him, and with His stripes we are healed."* The Beginning and End of our faith based on the plain Bible truth that *"Christ died for our sins,"* the Innocent for the guilty, the Eternal for the mortal, God for man, we not only overcome the fear of consequences, the dread of exposure, the panic of an enraged conscience, the furies of hell itself, but because we believe assuredly that *"the blood of Jesus Christ, His Son, cleanseth us from all sin,"* we know that our iniquities have been taken away forever. Pledged to the Savior, we have no reason to cringe before God, fearing that our transgressions may not have been completely forgiven; for the acceptance of divine approval was stamped upon our Lord's redemptive work when after His death-gasp, *"It is finished!"* He was gloriously resurrected from the dead on the third day. Nothing remains undone, nothing necessary for our salvation unfulfilled, not even the most insignificant part still to be accomplished. Judas could have been pardoned and restored had his remorse given way to a true, Christ-centered contrition; and if Jesus would have forgiven even His betrayer had that desperate disciple sought forgiveness in faith, you should believe that, since no sin could possibly be worse than Judas' treachery, the Savior has pardon, love, and peace for you. All you need—however scarlet or bloody your sins may be—after deep penetrating sorrow is sincere trust in the Lord Jesus—nothing more!

When Judas hanged himself and his disfigured body fell headlong to the ground, it was too late for repentance. Thank God, you still have a chance! But if you love your soul, do not postpone your contrite return to the Father! Don't figure on deathbed penitence or plan to live in sin until your last hour comes and then conveniently be converted to God! True, the thief on the cross was saved in the eleventh hour, showing that as long as there is life, it is not too late. A Christian physician in Maine who has systematically observed the dying moments of hundreds of sufferers, writes me to corroborate a happy certainty that often a last-moment word pointing to Christ can be of eternal blessing. Yet it is equally sure, as Christian ministers can testify, that in most cases dying unbelievers are not physically, mentally, spiritually, able to understand the offer of Christ's love. They have toyed with salvation, and it has slipped beyond their grasp!

Several years ago, reports from Russia announced that Red atheists would erect a gigantic, widely visible statue of Judas Iscariot to show their defiant rejection of Christ. I have not been able to ascertain how far they succeeded, nor does it matter. Some day the Soviets will learn the whole lesson of which even now they have apparently accepted the first chapters, that no country can long prosper in rebellion against the Almighty.

It is of more personal concern that you and I never altogether lose sight of Judas nor forget the lessons which his despair and suicide teach. Look at him once more in that fatal flight from the Temple, for in him we must see our own weaknesses mirrored; but while he ran from Christ, O God of all grace, help us hasten to the Savior with more than remorse—with real, Christ-directed repentance! Make us a truly contrite nation, in which devout citizens, though surrounded by the pomp and parade of the hour, humbly confess their faults and prayerfully seek divine guidance for the United States during the hazardous years ahead! Grant us truly penitent churches, keenly conscious of their reluctance to give everything in bringing the crucified Savior to masses in America! Bless us with repentant homes, so that grim despair may be banished from families united in trustful adoration of Christ! Give us, in our foremost benediction, truly contrite hearts, deep sorrow for our wrong, sincere resolve for the right, through faith in Jesus Christ our own and only Redeemer! We ask it in His name! Amen.

NOTES

Judas

Clarence Edward Noble Macartney (1879–1957)
ministered in Paterson, NJ, and Philadelphia, PA, before
assuming the influential pastorate of First Presbyterian
Church, Pittsburgh, PA, where he ministered for twenty-
seven years. His preaching especially attracted men, not
only to the Sunday services but also to his popular Tuesday
noon luncheons. He was gifted in dealing with Bible
biographies, and, in this respect, has well been called "the
American Alexander Whyte." Much of his preaching was
topical-textual, but it was always biblical, doctrinal and
practical. Perhaps his most famous sermon is "Come Before
Winter."

The sermon I have selected is taken from *Bible Epitaphs*,
reprinted in 1974 by Baker Book House.

Clarence Edward Noble Macartney

8
JUDAS

That he might go to his own place (Acts 1:25).

IN HIS ESSAY on "Persons One Would Wish to Have Seen," William Hazlitt makes Charles Lamb say: "I would fain see the face of him who, having dipped his hand in the same dish with the Son of Man, could afterward betray Him. I have no conception of such a thing, nor have I ever seen any picture that gave me the least idea of it."

No picture, Leonardo's, or that by any other artist, will ever tell the whole secret of Judas. Always he will be the enigma among the Apostles. In a way, he is the most definitely classified among the Twelve. He is dismissed with strong statements in the gospels, such as: "This he said. . . . because he was a thief, and had the bag"; "Satan entered into him"; "Judas, who betrayed Him." Yet, on the other side, how hard it is to conceive of what he did. His call to the discipleship, his companionship with Christ, his avarice, his treason, his remorse, his suicide, his predestination—all this, taken together in the same man, makes Judas a great mystery. Yet here is one thing, at least, that is said about Judas that we can all understand—"He went to his own place."

The disciples, one hundred and twenty of them, were met together in Jerusalem after the Ascension of their Lord. Peter, who presided, called on them to choose a successor to Judas. He rehearses the history of Judas, and how prophecy had been fulfilled in his tragic life and death. Nevertheless, he had been numbered with the disciples, and had obtained a part of their ministry. Peter then goes on to tell of the circumstances of the death of Judas, and the name that was given to the field in which he perished—Aceldama—the field of blood. Quoting Psalm 69 as a warrant for their procedure, Peter instructs the disciples to choose from two men who have been put forward a successor to Judas.

The remarkable thing about this address of Peter upon Judas is its noble restraint. He does not brand him as a thief, or a traitor, or a murderer, all of which he was; nor does he say of him, as John did, that "Satan entered into him." But he takes a last farewell of Judas with this single phrase, one that has a word of meaning in it; genuinely Christian, finely judicial, and, in this case, unutterably sad, "He went to his own place."

Peter did not say Judas went to hell, but to "his own place." At a summer conference, I once heard a speaker refer to the French skeptic, Voltaire, in these words, "After Voltaire had been dead and damned for a century." It fell with a harsh and unpleasant sound upon the ear, not because of any sympathy with Voltaire's hostility to Christianity, but because it seemed both un-Christian and presumptuous that even the best among men should speak of even the worst among men in such terms. It is one thing to declare the whole gospel of Christ and warn the impenitent of the danger of condemnation hereafter; but another thing to put one's self in the place of the supreme Judge and allot to one's fellow-beings their eternal destiny. How different, then, is the spirit of Peter when he comes to speak of Judas Iscariot. All that he says of him is this brief, yet solemn and searching word, "He went to his own place."

Whatever that place was, and we cannot think of it as a place of joy or peace, it was his own place that Judas had chosen. He had prepared for it, asked for it by the deeds of his life, and now he had entered into it. A solemn truth this, that we all choose our own place. As Judas built his house, so do we. The plan of it, the foundations, the furniture, the decorations—all are of our choosing and our design. Wherever the soul of Judas is tonight, he is in his own place.

Could it be possible to say to ourselves tonight anything that could be more arresting or searching than this? As you and I go through life we are preparing a place for ourselves. Every thought that passes swiftly through the chambers of the mind, every desire, every impulse, every word that escapes our lips, every secret and every public act, is a building of our final house and a choosing of our ultimate place. Both in this life and in the life to come, every man has a place which he chooses and creates for himself.

> The tissue of the life to be,
> We weave with colors all our own;
> And on the fields of destiny
> We reap as we have sown.

The High Place to Which All Men Are Called

Every man is called to a high place in life and in destiny, and, therefore, for all men such a place is possible. Judas did not occupy, finally, the high place to which he was called; but, as Peter says, fell away from it by transgression. Judas was called to follow Christ, called to be an apostle, called to be one of those who were to lay the foundations of the glorious temple of the Christian church. But from that place and office he fell away. He might have been remembered today as we remember Peter, or John, or Matthew, or St. Paul. Instead of that, whenever you pronounce the word Judas, you always add those four other sad words of the Gospels, "Who also betrayed him." Yet we must remember that one day Judas in the streets of Jerusalem, or along the highway, or by the Sea of Galilee, heard the voice of Jesus for the first time and was charmed by it. "Charmed to confess and follow on," Judas, one likes to think, was in the beginning a sincere and earnest follower of Christ. How sad and terrible, then, that other place which he finally chose in exchange for the place to which Christ had called him.

This is one of the great and stirring things about Christianity. It proclaims to man that there is a high place waiting for him and invites him to enter into it. When Saul, seeking his father's asses, came to inquire of the man of God, Samuel, in the town of Zuph, Samuel told him that his father's lost asses had been found. He was not to think any more about them, for something greater was now in view. The throne of Israel had been chosen for him. "For whom is all that is desirable in Israel?" Samuel said, "Is it not for thee and for all thy father's house?" In order that he might fit himself for his high office, God gave Saul another heart and turned him into another man. But Saul was not faithful to his place or to the God who had put him there. In spite of the tears and prayers of Samuel, in spite of the repeated warnings which came to him, Saul went at length to his own place. That was the burden of David's eloquent dirge and lament over Saul; the fact that he had come to a miserable end, slain and desecrated and mutilated by his foes, his bow and sword vilely cast away, "as though he had not been anointed with oil."

Ah, had we the eloquence of David, what dirges we could sing over those who fell away from the place which God intended for them and went instead to their own place. How often, could we know the history that lies hidden back of those faces which pass us on the street, they would speak to us in tones of sadness and warning of high places to which they had been called, but from which they have fallen away, perhaps despairing now of ever occupying the place they might have occupied and which God had chosen for them. One of the most moving things and most powerful things in all the writings of Charles Dickens is that passage in the *Tale of Two Cities* where he describes Sydney Carton ascending the stairs to his dismal lodgings and throwing himself with a flood of tears on his wretched bed as he thinks of what he might have done with his talents and the place he might have occupied, had he not cast it all away by the folly of his dissipation.

We Choose Our Own Place in This World

Peter was referring, of course, to the final place and destiny of Judas, when he said, "He went to his own place." But that final place was linked to, and was the result of, the place which Judas chose for himself here in this life. Not only, then, do we choose our final place and destiny, but we choose our own place in this world. Hour by hour, day by day, month by month, year by year, by every thought, desire, imagination, and act we choose a place for ourselves here and build for ourselves the house of the soul.

Imagine, if you will, two men as they go forth tomorrow morning to live the life of that one day. This man commences it without a prayer. Perhaps he ushers in the day with ugliness of temper and churlishness of behavior toward his wife or his family. When he goes to his work and place of business, he provokes others to wrath and resentment. When he speaks of others he does so with envy or malice. Thus pass the hours of the day, and when the man comes back to his home from which he started out in the morning, he comes a dreaded, rather than a welcome, visitor. That man has his place, and it is no uncertain place. Did he have all the gold of Croesus, his place is to be shunned by all who desire happiness and peace of mind. No one forced that place on him; he chose it and fashioned it from the earliest hour of the day until the last. The life that he has lived this day is now his companion for the night and a part of his nature for the morrow; and if, in addition to his harsh and unfriendly conduct there has been dishonesty or sinful indulgence, the man is not only robbed of the happiness and content that might have been his, but has for his companion that unpleasant visitor and that unceasing speaker, remorse. It is sad to see a man in such a place; but sadder still when one reflects that this is his own place, the very place that he has chosen.

How different from that man's place is the place of the man who greets the day with prayer and thanks unto God, and goes forth to his work assisting and encouraging others as he has opportunity, provoking not to wrath, but to good works; if meeting evil, returning good for evil, and forbearing in love; the man who hopes all things, believes all things, thinks no evil, rejoices not in iniquity, but rejoices in the truth; who suffers long and is kind. Night may find him weary, but content, for he is near to the fountain of love; and could we but see them, the angels of God wait upon him. If there is any sadness or heaviness in his heart, it is not because he thinks of those to whom he has been unjust or unkind, but because he grieves over the waywardness and sorrows and sins of others. He has chosen the more excellent way. He goes at the close of every day to his own place. We sometimes say that we are trying to "place" a man, to get the true conception of his personality and his character. Not always do we succeed in so doing, but always we do place ourselves. A man once said to me, a man who had fallen into great trouble and deep waters, "I was the architect of my own misfortune."

The Future Place

Judas went to his own place in the world to come. We would like to think of it as a place of happiness and worship; a place where the qualities of goodness and mercy, of love to God and charity to man which here survived the cold winter of this life, blossom and flower in all their beauty and fragrance; a place where memories of the days that were past sing their songs to cheer and gladden the heart; a place where the man who had lived upon the earth in a society where the good and evil mingled as the wheat and the tares, now has for his associates and companions only those who love the Lord and whose hearts are inclined to virtue. But, alas, when we put Judas in such a place we feel a strange incongruity in such an association. Judas in that place would be out of place. No, it was a different kind of place that Judas had chosen. Wise, chastened, and restrained, Peter makes no effort to lift the veil that covers the place of Judas, and all others who go out from the presence of the Lord. All that he says is, "He went to his own place."

We deal with a great mystery when we speak about the life to come, and there is some truth in what Dr. Brown in his *Religio Medici* says about our ignorance of that life, when he likens our conversation concerning it to the conversation of two unborn babes in the womb about the life of this world. Yet there are great principles which, upon the authority of Scriptures, we can lay down about that life to come. There is no reason to think that death, which solves so many problems and answers so many questions, makes any change in the moral character of the soul. Certainly the moral laws go on working there just as here. "He which is filthy, let him be filthy still: and he that is righteous, let him be righteous still." "As the tree falleth, so let it lie." There will be, no doubt, an infinite development of good for those who have chosen the good in this life, and likewise a development of evil, without the restraints and without the mitigations to the stings of remorse which obtain in this life.

The fact of the future life, and especially the fact of retribution in the future life, is a sadly neglected truth today. There are four great convictions—that there is a God; that there is a soul; that there is a life to come; and that there is judgment to come. You cannot dismiss retribution without dismissing God. It is not so much a truth that is brought to us from the outside, although revelation confirms it, but a deep instinct, a deep yearning, sometimes a deep dread, within the spirit of man. Yet it is a heavy subject, and the fate of the finally impenitent is one that we contemplate with awe, sometimes with deep questionings. For all who may be troubled on that subject, there is relief in these words of Peter about Judas; "He went to his own place," the place he had asked for and chosen in this life.

> Still, as of old, man by himself is priced;
> For thirty pieces Judas sold himself, not Christ.

Peter does not say that God sent Judas to that place, but that he went to it himself. Future retribution is not a capricious assignment of punishment; not so much what is done to a man by the great Judge, but what a man does to himself. "I myself am heaven and hell."

Judas went to his own place in spite of Christ, not because of Christ. All that Jesus said to the other disciples, save what he said after Judas had gone out into the night, he said to Judas also. Judas did not go unwarned to his doom. I like to think that the washing of his feet at the Supper by Jesus and the words of Jesus, "What thou doest, do quickly," and again, when he called him "Friend" in the Garden of Gethsemane, were last appeals to Judas to turn before it was too late. But Judas would not turn. I have no doubt that one of the chief elements of future punishment will be the consciousness a man has that what he now endures and suffers he chose for himself.

This is a solemn subject; but let us think, in closing, of another place, the place to which God calls us, the place for which every soul is fitted by reason of its creation in the image of God. "I go," said Christ, "to prepare a place for you." That is true, not only of the life to come, but of this present life. You can lose a place or an opportunity in this world, and it is gone forever. Someone else fills it; but God keeps your empty place waiting for you. As Jonathan said to David, "Thou shalt be missed, for thy place shall be empty."

Recently there was the story of a mother whose wayward son had gone out from her home. For years the mother had been waiting for him to return, and always at night there was a light burning in the window, and always in her heart, too, was burning the hope that her son would come home. The other day she died, and before her son came home. Now the light has gone out in the window. But, thanks be to God, the light in the window of our Father's house never goes out! Whenever the soul turns back to God, God sees us afar off, as in Christ's matchless tale, the father saw the returning and penitent son afar off, "and ran, and fell on his neck, and kissed him."

NOTES

Judas and the Priests—End of Evil Association

John Ker (1819–1886) is little known today, but in his day he was a respected preacher and professor of preaching and pastoral work at the United Free Church Seminary in Glasgow, Scotland. He published two volumes of sermons.

This one is from the *Sermons First Series*, published in Edinburgh in 1870 by Edmonston and Douglas.

John Ker

9

JUDAS AND THE PRIESTS—
END OF EVIL ASSOCIATION

Saying, I have sinned, in that I have betrayed the innocent
blood. And they said, What is that to us? See thou to that
(Matthew 27:4).

A CERTAIN GLOSS of interpretation has come in of late
upon the character of Judas, which tries to present it in a
milder light than that in which it was formerly regarded.

It is said that, after all, he may not have intended to
betray his Master to the death of the cross. He was one of
those Jews who believed very strongly in an earthly kingdom, and in the mission of Jesus of Nazareth to establish
it—an error which he shared with his fellow-disciples. He
was more impatient than the rest to bring Jesus to declare for it, and took a very rash step to gain his end. His
hope was that when Christ was in the hands of the high
priest and the Roman governor, He would throw away all
reserve, and come forth as a conqueror and king. It was,
in short, not the *money* Judas looked to, but the *idea*. He
was not, in the proper sense, guilty of treachery, but of a
mistake, and merely sought to thrust Christ from the
temple pinnacle, in the belief that He would rise to a
loftier position.

However this particular comment may have been intended, it is one of a class which begins by effacing what
it reckons dark spots in the Bible, and ends by darkening
the bright. There are depths and heights in the mystery
of sin and salvation which go together, and whatever takes
away from the possibility of the soul's fall weakens its
capacity for ascent. If all sin could be shown to be only a
mistake of judgment, there would be no need of Christ
and redemption through His blood, and with the ineffable
sorrows would depart the infinite joys.

The attempt may seem ingenious, but in some things ingenuity is the worst token of truth. The Bible has no doubt still much to be found out by diligent search, but in an estimate of character, in the very center of New Testament history, the immense probability is that the judgment of centuries and of the church universal is right.

It is a gloss that is entirely out of keeping with the drift of the Gospel narrative. The character of Judas is streaked long before with the sin which led to his final crime. He murmured at the token of affection which was given to Christ, because he wished to turn it to his own covetous advantage. He was a thief and he had the bag, and hypocritically put forward the poor as a pretext to gain his own selfish ends. When he went out on his treacherous errand it is said, "Satan entered into him," and though this has been compared with our Lord's word to Peter (Matt. 16:23), "Get thee behind me, Satan," the expression of fact in a calm narrative is surely very different from the indignant rejection which our Lord applied, not to the apostle, but to his suggestion. When Judas went out on his errand he went alone, as feeling that he had no sympathy in the hearts of the rest. He chose night and secrecy for his bargain. He covenanted to take money, *and did take it*, and if the amount was paltry for so great a crime, it proves not that there was any higher motive, but that covetousness can bring down the soul to the most miserable price.

Much has been founded on the expression, "Judas, which had betrayed him, when he saw that he was condemned" (Matt. 27:3)—as if he had expected that Christ would free Himself before it came so far; but the remorse of Judas at this moment can be perfectly explained by the full consequences of his act now looking him in the face. It is the murderer's horror when the deed is committed and *cannot be undone*—that awful revulsion which, among all calculations, is never reckoned on.

Moreover, if he had expected Christ to free Himself, as this theory of Judas affirms, his despair should not have commenced so early. Judas should not have ceased to hope until the crucifixion was complete. Many of Christ's past interpositions had taken place in extremity, and why not now! It is clear that it was not a mistake but a crime that was revealed by the lightning flash thrown in upon his soul. His words prove this: "I have sinned, in that I have betrayed the innocent blood." To tone them down to the discovery of a misapprehension is to rob them of all their meaning, and of that lesson, so deep and far-reaching, which the church of Christ has always read in this event—the greatest sin lying like a black shadow beneath the world's brightest light.

The chief purpose for which we wish to use this passage is to show the end to which association in sin conducts. Men join hand in hand for a wicked object, out of which they hope for common profit. For a while the alliance lasts, and evil seems to have its laws and power of coherence as well as good. But conflicting interests rise, and then the nature of the union is apparent. Sin began by severing the bond between man and his Maker, and what other bond can henceforth have any permanence! If left to do its will, it would disintegrate God's universe into atoms of selfishness. While the Cross of Christ was being raised as the center of spiritual attraction—divine self-sacrifice—here, around its base, and in wonderful connection with it, sin was permitted to exhibit its character of repulsion in the darkest colors. There are two instructive sides in the separation which takes place, and we shall consider them in order—Judas and his state of mind; the chief priests and their conduct toward him.

Judas, and the State of Mind to Which He Is Brought

The most striking way, perhaps, in which we can consider this, is to attempt to trace in Judas that feature of sin to which we have made reference—its tendency to isolate the man who perseveres in it, until he is left all alone. He begins in the *guilt* of selfishness and ends in its utter *solitude*.

The first effect of his sin *is separation from human companionship*. Up to this time, he had lived in the outward fellowship of Christ and the other chosen eleven. It may seem strange to us that Christ should ever have admitted Judas to that number. The only reasonable account of it which we can form is this, that our Lord acted by Judas as He did by all the rest. He accepted him on the ground of a profession which was consistent as far as human eye could see. Christ Himself received members into His church as He intended that we should receive them—for, had He used His divine omniscience in His judgments, the whole structure of his life would have been out of our reach as an example; Judas accordingly entered among the apostles, because, in all outward things, and even in some inward convictions, he was like them. He came under the same influences—listened to the same invitations and warnings—and they were meant as truly for Judas as for the rest. It would have gladdened the heart of Christ had Judas yielded to the voice of mercy.

It is not any question for us how then the Savior could have suffered for the sins of men, any more than it is a question how the history of the world would proceed without the sinful deeds which are permitted by God and gathered by Him into the final result. The plan of the universe, in its lowest or its highest part, does not rest on the doom of any man to be a sinner. God forbid! There are manifold doors in the divine purpose which God may open or shut as He pleases, but there is one always shut—that God should tempt any man to evil—and there is one forever open—that He wills not the death of the sinner, but that he should turn and live. Whatever difficulties may be in these questions of freedom and decree, we can never permit the speck of one to touch the divine purity and mercy. If Judas had come, he would have been welcomed as any other.

But he did not come, and gradually the gulf in his secret soul must have widened between him and those with whom he outwardly walked. He was with them, but not of them, and slowly this must have become apparent to his own consciousness. Next in grievousness to the havoc which a hidden sin works in a man's nature is the separation of his heart from the fellowship of the good around him—the sense of shame and degradation with which he must compare their estimate of him with what he really is. He is held to them by custom and repute—sometimes by a feeling of the needed check which their society exercises over him—and yet he is more and more repelled by the want of sympathy and by the necessity for hypocrisy which becomes every day more irksome.

Yet so long as the great overt act was not committed, Judas could continue in the circle of his former friends. Happy influences were still breathing around him; he felt that a change of course was yet open, and he soothed his conscience perhaps with the thought of one day taking it. If any man is in this position, let him not delay. It is something to hold on to the society of the true and good; but it is always dishonorable to do it falsely, and the connection may be broken at any moment if we do not join them in our inmost soul.

The sin of Judas, long cherished and slowly growing, broke out at last with terrible and open power, and changed his whole position. It is a great mistake to say that sin in the heart is the very same as sin thrown into a deliberate and daring act. They are in the same line, as our Lord has taught us, but the external act gives evil a power which it had not before, and which may prove fatally destructive. It is like a combustible material, which, if once exploded, may leave the man's nature a shattered and hopeless wreck. To repress sin from the actual life is something—only let it not stop there, else it is a constant deception and danger.

When Judas let the character which he had slowly formed go out into his terrible treachery, he felt as if a bridge were broken behind him. In that bewildering night in the garden, he was swept from the side of Christ, and only then did he begin to realize what he had done and what he had lost. He could no more look upon the face of the Master he had sold. The trustful happy circle of the Twelve was broken, and he, of them all, was left utterly alone. However they might meet in secret, and fearfully, to speak of their past and their future—of the death of their love and hope—he felt that he had no more part nor lot among them. There is not any distance in space or time—not any change in circumstances—which will so cut a man off from his fellowmen as one sin will do. But it will generally be found that this sin is the outcome of a secret life which stands discovered by it. It is God's way of letting us see, even now, what final judgment will disclose—the revelation of an utter incompatibility, which makes a man seek no more a fellowship where he never had a true share.

In his terrible solitude, Judas turned to his employers and accomplices. It could scarcely be in the hope of forming any new ties. Friendships were not at present in his thoughts, and not to be looked for in that circle. There was the pressure of despair on him—the sting that sometimes drives the criminal to proclaim his sin that others may know the worst of him. The secret burden of a crime may prove so intolerable that publicity will feel almost like pardon.

There may have been, too, the prompting which sometimes leads a man to seek any human presence as a relief from the terror of his own thoughts. He could not expect that the priests would relax their hold on Christ for any confession of his, but he may have faintly looked for some word which could help him against his own bitter accusations. But here the gulf of separation opens again. The chilling question, "What is that to us?" and the look which must have accompanied it, told him that, as he had cut himself off from the good, he was cast off by the wicked. He had served their purpose, and is thrown away like a broken tool.

Men have been able to dig for each other deep dark dungeons, far from man's face and God's pleasant sunlight, but there is no fearful pit of solitude like that which a soul can sink for itself. It may be more rare that it takes the form of a crime, like that of Judas, which sets him separate, like a wonder and a terror; but all sin has this quality in its nature. It divides from those whose friendship can be trusted, and it can form no other tie which will endure.

The next thing to be remarked of the sin of Judas is that it brought him to a state *where he was deserted by himself.* We may call a man self-deserted when he cannot be alone with his own thoughts. We have each of us a personality which we feel to be our real self and which lives on amid all change and circumstance. But with this, there is a circle of thoughts and feelings different from this self and yet inseparably connected with it. They are the inner home which every soul is engaged in fashioning for itself and which is destined to be its eternal dwelling place. As long as we can keep company with its memories and hopes, we are never in utter solitude. When we have to turn away from it, we are alone indeed.

Let us say here, that there are some who do turn away from it without being in the worse case. A calamity may have crazed the brain, or a morbid specter looked in on the heart and jarred the sweet strings of their nature, and alienated them from life and self as Job seems to have been. We all know when the wrong lies, not in the book of the soul, but in the man's disordered reading of it; and how sure we may be that, if not here, yet hereafter, he will be made to see light in God's light. The jarred strings which have sent forth this temporary discord will give out sweeter music at last for the strain put upon them.

The terrible self-desertion is when conscience is roused, and makes the thoughts intolerable because of the presence of a sin which cannot be got rid of. Backward, forward, upward, this meets the man wherever he turns his look, and his feeling is that which the poet has given to the apostate angel, "Me miserable, which way shall I fly!"

It may be seldom in this world that one is brought to such blackness of darkness, but it is certain that every sin he consciously commits is making him less able to keep company with himself. He may not take note of it at the time, but his conscience is doing the work of the hand on Belshazzar's wall. It is writing down terrible words, and such a force can be put into them that when they are set in order before his eyes, his knees shall smite together, and he will seek to escape anywhere from his own thoughts.

Further, it is to be observed that Judas *was deserted by*

the tempter and the bribe—deserted, at least, so far as the
false strength is concerned which had hitherto sustained
him. It is the distinct teaching of the Gospels that, besides the chief priests, there was another influence at
work outside Judas—the enemy who seduced man to sin
at first, and who still is engaged in the work of temptation.

The kingdom of evil, as well as that of good, has a
personal head. That he should have the power of tempting is no more strange than that human spirits should
possess it. He can no more compel than they, and he
gains in influence only as we yield him place. The experience of many temptations points to such a power in operation. There is a halo cast around worldly objects and a
glow of passionate attractiveness breathed into them,
which are not in themselves, and which can scarcely come
from the mind that looks on them. Crimes are committed
and souls bartered for such miserable bribes that to the
rational spectator it is utterly unnatural, and the man
himself wonders at it when the delirium is past. Our
great dramatic poet has seized this feature of sin—this
strange *residuum* in temptation, which indicates an extra-
human agency—and has set it down to those unseen powers of evil which "palter with us in a double sense." It
does not diminish any man's responsibility, but it should
increase his vigilance. Not only are these powers unable
to constrain the will, they have no influence of seduction,
no delusive atmosphere at command, where the heart has
not prepared itself for it, by cherishing the sin long and
deeply.

Judas had made ready his own nature for the tempter.
He, and none but he, could have rendered himself capable
of yielding. And now that he has yielded, the power at
work becomes apparent in the disenchantment which fol-
lows. The seducer, in this form at least, leaves him, and
withdraws the allurement of his promise. There is something wonderful, if it were not so common, in the sight of
this fortitude of the transgressor failing in the very moment of success, in the sudden change in value of what he
had coveted an hour before, until the silver, which was so

dear, eats his flesh as it were fire, and he casts it from him like a viper that has stung his hand. It is the act of a treacherous ally who has lured his sinful victim to his selected place and then deserts him in the instant of his ruin.

Whether men will admit the agency of an unseen tempter or not, they must grant that a sinful object has a very different look before and after possession—that in the hour of promised enjoyment it shrinks and shrivels, or becomes hideous and loathsome. Whatever we deduct from the influence of Satan we must attribute in a corresponding measure to that of sin, for the fact remains that the powers of evil, sooner or later, abandon the man who has sold himself to them. They promise what they never pay, and buoy up with a false courage which fails at the moment it is wanted. After sin has made a man so that he cannot look steadily into his own soul, it ends by destroying his enjoyment in that fictitious world of pleasure for which it has induced him to sell all that is divine and real. It cheats him of the substance for a shadow, and of that shadow it robs him, or changes it into a frightful phantom from which he would escape if he could—as Judas from the hire of his treachery.

We have seen how sin separates a man from the friendship of the good, from the sympathy even of the wicked, from fellowship with his own thoughts, from pleasure in the thing he coveted; and now we come to the last feature, *the separation it effects between the soul and God.* The first step in sin is such a separation begun; but there seems to be a stage which a man may reach in this world when nothing will induce him to turn his face to Him whom he has abandoned. If a man under the overwhelming conviction of guilt can still look to God, it makes his sin seem more sinful, but it makes the thought of it more supportable, for it gives him the view of mercy and reparation. There are no straits in guilt where there is not help in God, if the man will only hope. But if sin has gained such power over him that, though he feels its bitter fruit, it is less painful to him than the presence and the thought of God, what is to be done? That which is reviving light to others is to such a man consuming fire, and flight from God's face is sought by him as a relief and escape.

While the man maintains this position, the nature within him cannot be changed, and in that nature lies his misery. The terrible hardness which makes remorse different from repentance arises from the view of sin without the true view of God. It is a fearful truth that there may be the most bitter and tormenting sense of guilt without any real godly repentance for it. The heart of stone may be crushed and remain stone in its every fragment; it can only be melted when the love of God is suffered to shine on it. And if the man has so depraved his nature that God with all His love has become a distaste and revulsion to him, and evil with all its misery less intolerable, what are we to think of it? It might seem utterly impossible that any being in God's universe could ever reach such a state if we had not instances of it, no, if we had not the proof of it in our own nature. Whenever any one of us, in the presence of a sinful object, or after a sin has been committed, strives to put away the thought of God—when we do not like to retain Him in our knowledge—we are touching the edge of this terrible darkness, and we may have some idea how men may come at last to love that darkness rather than the light.

These are subjects very painful, but very needful, and they are forced upon our consideration in such a case as this. It is of all things most certain that a soul living consciously in sin is living without God, and to be without God is to be without hope. This, too, is certain, that the longer a man thus lives the more does absence from God deepen the sense of dislike, and the more difficult and improbable will be his return. The thought of this may not trouble some very much at present, because they feel as if they can live without God in a very pleasurable way, and they do not see why they should ever have a greater necessity for Him. They can put friendships and occupations in his room, and contrive to forget Him. But when these pass, as pass they must, and perish like flowers on the edge of a gulf, the awful depth of the chasm will be seen. When fold after fold which now closes the eye of the soul is torn off, and it is compelled to look on eternal realities, how will it stand the gaze? This loss of God must then be felt to be that loss of the soul of which the Savior speaks, when he asks, What shall a man give in exchange for it? And when He who made the soul, and loved it so much, puts the issue before us so solemnly, should it not bring us seriously to question ourselves, and to resolve to give place to nothing that will cloud our clear view of God, and never to betray Christ and the homage we owe Him for the whole world?

The Chief Priests and Their Conduct

In the case of Judas we see sin when it has reached its close; here we can perceive some of its features when still in the strength of its course.

The first thing that strikes us on their part is, *their disregard for their instrument when their purpose is gained.* Judas had served their end in putting Christ into their power quietly and securely, so as to avoid the hazard of public insurrection. And now for the traitor himself they have no further concern. They could not but see his agony in his face and bearing, an agony which was haunting him without respite, and fast making life intolerable. But for all this they have no regard. They could relieve his anguish only by releasing Christ, and this would be to surrender the object for which they had made use of Judas. If they had let Christ go free from any such motive, they would have been different men from what they were. Even Judas himself could not complain. He had tried to make his use of them as they of him, and there was no pretense of principle or affection on either side. They had kept their share of the contract, and he must abide by his. This is the remorseless logic which belongs to these cases, and among such men it is all-powerful. It raises a feeling of commiseration for the poor outcast wretch to see him so repulsed. Had he gone so to Christ, he would have been otherwise received.

That this is the natural end of all these associations there can be little doubt—of all alliances that are made for mutual aid in the pursuit of revenge or unhallowed ambition, of unjust gain or sinful pleasure. Let us admit that there will appear sometimes in the worst of men a remnant of human feeling which casts back a fragment of pity to a fallen accomplice, yet it is given only when it does not interfere with the purpose for which they sought his help. They love that purpose better than him, and when it is selfish, and wickedly selfish, we can easily calculate how far their sympathy will go, how little sacrifice it will make, and how soon it will weary of that little. We know well enough, too, how seldom any glimmerings of commiseration rise in such alliances, and how the contract is that of the wolves of the forest, which devour their fallen companions and continue the chase.

"And the chief priests took the silver pieces." It was like stripping a dead comrade. They had not the natural feeling to let the wretched hire lie, but they must lift it for a use of their own. Let this be learned, that if any friendship is to be formed that will stand us in stead in time of trial, it need not be sought among bad men consorting for unprincipled ends. Under the courtesies which have been established by conventionalism, or among the excitements of social pleasure this may be forgotten, but the first stress will lay bare the hollowness of such friendships and show what bitter enemies confront one another when wicked men are separated by selfish purposes.

The next thing in the conduct of the chief priests is their attempt *to shake off the responsibility of the common act.* Judas confesses in his agony the entire innocence of his Master. Christ was guiltless of any such design as they charged him with—of self-seeking or earthly ambition—and they knew it as well as Judas. It was because He refused to yield to this that He was both betrayed and condemned. It was because Judas had given up any hope of worldly gain, through his kingdom, that he had sold Him to them. And now, not only Christ's guiltlessness of the charge, but His spotless and loving character—the good he had received at His hands, and never evil—the gentle considerateness—the unwearied patience—the pitying tenderness He had shown him and his fellow-disciples—rose up before the soul of His betrayer, and smote him with unutterable remorse. No one word, no one act, could he call up that would help his own thoughts to justify his treachery. And when the consciousness of his guilt is crushing him, his associates refuse all share in it. "What is that to us?" If Christ is innocent it is not their concern. The traitor who knew Him so well should have thought of this when he surrendered Him. And in this, they touch the very point which stung Judas to the quick, the one thing which made his guilt blacker than theirs. He knew Christ better, and sinned more against the purity and love of His nature. There is no more deplorable fall than in the case of those who have been most in Christ's company, and no sorer blow than when a hard worldling strikes an apostate Christian professor.

This attempt to shake off responsibility is a very common feature in all evil associations. There comes an ultimate and dreadful condition of mind, when, as in the case of Judas, all refuges of lies are swept away, when nothing but guilt, guilt without contrition, stares the man in the face. But there is a state of things on the way to this through which Judas, too, may have passed—the effort to shake off all share in the guilt and to cast it on others. The first compact of evil in the world manifests it—"the woman that thou gavest to be with me"—"the serpent beguiled me, and I did eat." Sometimes it is an attempt to put down an upbraiding conscience, sometimes to outface an accusing accomplice. But this is certain, that one of the punishments in concerted sin is mutual recrimination, and that the weakest are denied not only pity but ordinary justice.

The last feature we mention in their conduct is *that they end their sinful compact with a taunt.* "What is that to us? see thou to that." It is a sneer at his being too late in coming to the knowledge of Christ's innocence. This view of the matter should have suggested itself sooner. It is undisguised contempt for his helplessness. They despised him all along, and now they can show it. And there is probably an intended derision of his remorse. There are some men who, whether from a harder physical nature, or from the application of mental opiates, can drug their conscience until the stings of it in others are regarded as signs of feebleness. They look on the man who suffers from them as a deserter and a coward. It is difficult to say whether the meanness of sin is most revealed in Judas or in them—in his degradation, or their spurning of him. A generous man can use sarcasm—it is the scorn felt by a true nature for what is base, but a sneer has always a vein of the ignoble in it, and a sneer at a fallen accomplice belongs to natures of the lowest grade. Some find it hard to face the serpent's hiss of hatred, but here is something worse to endure—its hiss of scorn. Better by infinite meet the ridicule of sinners for not joining them while we have a good conscience, than end by being subjected to their taunts when we feel they are deserved.

Yet before leaving these men, let us be sure of this, that though they might disown responsibility they could not destroy it. A man may stop his chronometer in the night, but he cannot arrest the sunrise. The time shall come when *they too must see to it,* and the innocent blood find another voice than in the remorse of Judas. The two sides of sinful companionship we have been contemplating show us two stages in sin, the one its full career, the other its close. As long as men are in the pursuit of an object, they may be able, with the aid of passion, to stifle conscience, but when the object is reached, and the value deliberately counted—the thirty pieces of silver for which a Savior has been sold—conscience can begin to strike the balance. The heat and halo of the chase are over, and the net result can be reckoned, at least on one side, the miserable gain, if not the infinite loss. So it is with the betrayer, and so it must be, by and by, with those who hired him. They may meanwhile out brave Judas, but they have to meet God. And, let us think of it—the poisoned arrow a man uses may wound himself. The sneer is always on the way to the remorse. They have both the same hard bitterness in them—the same want of God's love. No more, as their taunts now pierce him, he may turn around and reach them. Mutual reproach is one of the miseries of confederate sin when it closes. On one side the burden of sin has a dreadful solitude about it. "Every man must bear his own burden"—"See thou to that." And yet, on the other side, there is a fearful companionship, for one sinner takes up this taunt against another. May not this be the meaning of that solemn sentence—"Gather ye the tares, and *bind them in bundles* to burn them"?

In what we have said, we have been looking chiefly at the end of sin and sinful association in this world. If we had no other view of it, there is enough to fill us with fear and awe—that sin cherished in the soul should so ruin human nature and leave it a wreck of guilt and agony. While the other disciples stumbled to rise, because truth and love to the Son of God were in their hearts, and while they grew up to that self-sacrifice and nobility of soul which make their names mingle in our thoughts with that Name which is above every name, the traitor's has gone out and down among men as a thing of loathing and horror, and is the perpetual warning of the awful catastrophe to which sin, cherished in the soul, at last may lead. There is surely no prayer which better befits us in such a review than the psalmist's: "Who can understand his errors? cleanse thou me from secret faults. Keep back thy servant also from presumptuous sins; let them not have dominion over me: then shall I be upright, and I shall be innocent from the great transgression."

It is scarcely possible, when we have such a case before us, to avoid thinking also of the future world. This matter is no subject for passion or threat, but for serious thought each one with himself. The New Testament has an expression concerning Judas which is as practical as profoundly solemn—"*He went to his own place*" (Acts 1:25). In the eternal world every man has *his place*, and it is *his own*. No other can make it, and no other can occupy it for him. Whatever may be in it outwardly, its essence lies in his own soul and in the condition to which he has brought it. Here, in the last issue, consists his misery or joy, for only through his soul can his share be measured in the universe of God and in God Himself.

And God has made the man's own soul witness and judge over itself. This difference only will exist between

the present and the future that then—confronted with
the eternal laws of truth and justice—the witness shall
have no power of false testimony and the judge be unable
to use favor or sophistry. We may say, that by thus lodg-
ing the decision in every man's conscience, God has put it
out of His own power to act with partiality, and put it out
of our power to charge Him with it. If the conscience could
truly charge the Supreme Lawgiver with injustice, it may
be affirmed with all reverence that this would sustain it
against the wrong. Men shall take their own place in the
spiritual universe as bodies take their place in the natural—by the power of gravitation which is in them—nearer
God or further from Him, as they have impressed the
character upon themselves, and in nearness will lie life
and peace—in distance, death and misery.

It may be a congratulation with some that such cases
as that of Judas are exceptional, and, that without having
decidedly chosen for God, they have nothing of the blackness of the betrayer nor the malignity of his accomplices.
Let this be meanwhile granted, and let it be admitted
that in the future world there must be infinite gradations
on either side. To deny this, and to make only two unre-
lieved colors, would be untruthful to God's justice and to
the plainest lessons of the Bible. But let anyone ask himself if he could think it well to remain on the same side
with Judas, only not so deep in degradation? If it were
possible, could he be contented with some borderland between God and sin? The history of the Cross of Christ,
which is so wonderful a touchstone of human nature, shows
us, in the person of Pilate, one who attempted it. If any
man could have escaped taking a part between Christ
and His enemies, it might have been Pontius Pilate. He
was a heathen who might excuse himself from Jewish
questions, and he was reared among the conflicting skep-
ticisms of his day in such a way that his question, "What
is truth?" appeared hopeless of an answer. But with all
his struggles he was forced to take a side. He might wash
his hands before the multitude and say, "See ye to it," but
the stain of Christ's blood is on them yet, and he stands a
miserable example of that weak and fancied neutrality

which can never be sustained! If God had no claims, and sin were not already master of our nature, neutrality might be spoken of, but he who chooses it as things are, elects to remain a rebel. If the Son of God had not entered the world with His summons to return to allegiance, the case might have been, at least, more doubtful; but now we must either be among those who gather to the side of divine Truth when it rises on the cross into the form of love, or take our part with the chief priests and Judases who buy and sell Him, and the Pilates who think they can stand by and harmlessly hold the scales.

What a deep ground of thankfulness should it be to all of us, that the standard which calls us to take a side holds out a free and full pardon to the worst of rebels—to the betrayers of the Son of God, and to His murderers, if they will but turn to Him! The death of Christ, which is such a revelation of human character, is a revelation still more of God's mercy. The death rises into a sacrifice, the crime discloses an atonement, and if those who joined in the treason would have but looked on Him whom they pierced, all would have been forgiven and the abundance of sin swallowed up in the abundance of grace.

From whatever is doubtful and mysterious, let us turn to this—the light which shines in darkness. Let us be afraid not so much of the punishment of sin as of sin itself feeling that it bears its sting in its own bosom, and that, if there be in any child of man the desire to be freed from it, he is welcomed by the full heart of God drawing near to us in that Redeemer who is able to save to the uttermost all those that come unto God through Him.

Melting the Betrayer

Robert Murray McCheyne (1813–1843) is one of the brightest lights of the Church of Scotland. Born in Dundee, he was educated in Edinburgh and licensed to preach in 1835. For a brief time, he assisted his friend Andrew A. Bonar at Larbert and Dunipace. In 1836 he was ordained and installed as pastor of St. Peter's Church, Dundee, where he served until his untimely death two months short of his thirtieth birthday. He was known for his personal sanctity and his penetrating ministry of the Word, and great crowds came to hear him preach. *The Memoirs of and Remains of Robert Murray McCheyne*, by Andrew Bonar, is a Christian classic that every minister of the gospel should read.

This sermon is taken from *The Additional Remains of the Rev. Robert Murray McCheyne*, published in 1846 in Edinburgh by William Oliphant and Company.

Robert Murray McCheyne

10

MELTING THE BETRAYER

When Jesus had thus said, He was troubled in spirit, and testified, and said, Verily, verily, I say unto you, that one of you shall betray me (John 13:21).

THERE ARE MANY excellent and most Christian men who think that the feast of the Lord's Supper should never be sullied or interrupted by allusions to those who may be eating and drinking unworthily. They think that when men have, by their own solemn act and deed, deliberately seated themselves at the table of the Lord—that table to which none but believers in Jesus are invited—they think that, for the time being, at least, it is the part of that charity which hopes all things, to address them as if all were the genuine disciples of Jesus, and children of God. These good men know well that there are always many intruders into that holy ordinance; they know that many come from mere custom, and a sense of decency, and from a dislike to be marked out as openly irreligious and profane; and though they feel, in addressing the whole mass as Christians, many a rise of conscience within, many a sad foreboding that the true guests may be the little flock, while the intruders may be the vast majority. Yet they do not feel themselves called upon to disturb the enjoyment of the believing flock, however few they may be, by insinuating any such dark suspicion that there may be some there who have already sold their Lord for their sins—some who, though they may eat bread with Him, yet lift up the heel against Him.

Now a most complete answer to the scruples of these good men is to be found in the example of our blessed Lord. In that night, so much to be remembered, in which He instituted the Lord's Supper—a night in which nothing but kindness and tenderness flowed from His blessed

135

lips—we find that no fewer than five times over did He begin to speak about His betrayer. In many respects that was the most wonderful evening that ever was in the world, and that upper room in Jerusalem the most wonderful room that ever was in the world. Never did the shades of evening gather around a more wonderful company—never did the walls of an upper chamber look upon so wonderful a scene.

Three strange events were crowded into that little space. First, there was the washing of the disciples' feet—the Lord of glory stooping as a servant to wash the feet of poor worms! Second, there was the last Passover—eating of the lamb and the bitter herbs—which had been the memorial of the dying Savior to all believing Jews, but which was now to come to an end. Third, there was the first Lord's Supper—the breaking of bread and pouring out of wine, and the giving and the receiving of it; which was to be the memorial of His dying love even to the end of the world. Oh! what an assemblage of love was here—what a meeting together of incidents, each one more than another picturing forth the inexpressible love of Jesus! Oh! what an awfully tender hour was this! Oh! what an awfully tender joy was now thrilling through the bosoms of His believing disciples! Oh! brethren, what an exalting gladness would now fill the bosom of the courageous Peter! What an adoring love the breast of the Israelite indeed, the simple-hearted Nathanael! And what a breathing of unspeakable affection in the heart of the beloved John, as he leaned on the dear Savior's bosom! Oh! who would break in on such an hour of holy joy with harsh and cruel words about the betrayer? Who would dare to ruffle the calm tranquillity of such a moment by one word of dark suspicion? Hush! brethren, it is the Savior that speaks: *"Verily, verily, I say unto you, that one of you shall betray me."*

I trust, then, my friends, you see plainly, from the example of our blessed Lord, that the awfully solemn warning of the text, instead of being a rash and unwarrantable intrusion upon the joyous feelings with which every true disciple should encompass the table of the Lord, is, of all other Scriptures, the most appropriate, and the most like what Jesus would have us to say upon this solemn occasion. It is not, then, with the harshness of unfeeling man, but it is with the tenderness of the compassionate Jesus that we repeat these words in your hearing: Verily, verily, I say unto you, that one of you shall betray me."

There is a cruel kindness, almost too cruel, one would think, for this cruel world, which is sometimes practiced by the friends of a dying man, when from day to day they mark the approaches of death upon his pallid cheek, and yet they will not breathe a whisper of his danger to him. They flatter him with murderous lies—that he is getting better and will yet see many days when his days are numbered. But ten thousand times more cruel, more base and unfeeling would that minister be who, set over you by God to care for your never-dying souls, should yet look upon those of you who surround so willingly the table of the Lord, but whose whole life, and walk, and conversation, proclaim you to be the betrayers of that Lord, and not once lift up the warning cry: "Ye are not all clean. Verily, verily, I say unto you, that one of you shall betray me."

Question: What could be Christ's reason for so often and so solemnly speaking of His betrayer?

Answer: I can see no other reason for it but that He might make one last effort to melt the heart of His betrayer.

Doctrine: Christ is earnestly seeking the salvation of those unconverted persons who sit down at His table.

There are two arguments running through the whole of this scene, by means of which Jesus tried to melt the betrayer. First, *His perfect knowledge of him.* As if He had said: I know thee, Judas; I know your whole life and history; I know that you have always been a thief and a traitor; I know that you have sold me for thirty pieces of silver; I know all your plans and all your crimes. In this way He tried to awaken the traitor—to make him feel himself a lost sinner. Second, *His anxious love for him.* As if He had said: I love you, Judas; I have left the bosom of the Father just for lost sinners like you; I pitied you before the world was; I am quite willing still to be a Savior to you. In this way He tried to win the traitor—to draw him to Himself.

Christ Knows Judas' Whole Heart

All the Savior's dealings with Judas were intended to convince him that He knew his whole heart: "I know you, Judas, and all your crimes."

1. This was plainly His intention when washing the disciples' feet and telling them, that if they be bathed in His blood, they need nothing more than to have their feet washed—their daily sins wiped off daily: "Ye are clean every whit." He then adds, but *Ye are not all clean.*" This was evidently intended as a hint to Judas, to awaken his guilty conscience.

2. And then, when He had sat down again, to partake of the Passover with them, and had sent around the cup of the Passover, saying, as we are told in Luke: "Take this and divide it among yourselves," He would not let Judas slumber, as if He were unknown to him; but declares more plainly than before: "I know whom I have chosen; but that the Scripture may be fulfilled, He that eateth bread with me hath lifted up his heel against me." This was evidently intended as a plainer intimation to Judas that, however concealed he might be to others, he was naked and laid open to the eyes of the Savior, with whom he had to do.

3. And, *thirdly,* when He was about to put the bread and wine into their hands, to institute the holy ordinance of the Supper, He would not do it without a still more convincing proof to the conscience of Judas that He knew him perfectly: "As they did eat, he said, Verily I say unto you, that one of you shall betray me: and they were exceeding sorrowful, and began every one of them to say unto him, Lord, is it I? And he answered, He it is that dippeth his hand with me in the dish; he it is that betrayeth me. And Judas answered and said, Lord, is it I? He said unto him, Thou hast said." Here we find the Savior no longer deals in hints and intimations, but tells him plainly he is the man. Oh! my friends, if we did not

know the deceitfulness of the natural heart, how it evades the most pointed declarations of the Word, we would be amazed that the heart of Judas was not overwhelmed with the conviction: "Thou, Lord, sees me. But no; the arrows of the Savior, so faithfully directed, yet strike off from his heart as from a flinty rock, and Judas sits still at the table of the Lord, still secure, to receive with his bloody hands (those hands which so lately had received the thirty pieces of silver, the price of blood) the symbols of the Savior's broken body, which he himself was to betray. Ah! my friends, are there no hearts here like Judas', from which the plainest arrows of conviction, having written on them: "Thou art the man," glance off, without even wounding? Are there none of you who sit Judas-like, with unclean hands to receive the memorials of the Savior whom you are betraying?

4. And last of all, when the feast of love was over—when Judas, with unaffected conscience, had swallowed down the bread and wine, whose sacred meaning he did not, and could not, know—Jesus, deeply affected, "being troubled in spirit," made one last effort, more pointed than all that went before, to thrust the arrow of conviction into the heart of Judas. When the beloved John, lying on Jesus' breast, said unto him: "Lord, who is it? Jesus answered, He it is to whom I shall give a sop when I have dipped it. And when he had dipped the sop, he gave it" (unseen, it would appear by all the rest) "to Judas Iscariot, the son of Simon. And Jesus said unto him, That thou doest, do quickly."

That this pointed word of the Lord was intended to awaken Judas, and for no other reason, is plain from the fact that "no man at the table knew for what intent he spake this unto him. For some of them thought, because Judas had the bag, that Jesus had said unto him, Buy those things that we have need of against the feast; or, that he should give something to the poor." So secretly, but so powerfully, did the Savior seek to awaken the slumbering conscience of the traitor. How was it possible he could miss the conviction that Christ knew all the thoughts and intents of his heart? How did he not fall down and confess that God was in him of a truth? Or like the Samaritan woman: "Come, see a man that told me all things that ever I did. Is not this the Christ?" But Satan had his dark mysterious hold upon him; and not more dark was the gloomy night which met his eyes as he issued forth upon his murderous errand than was the dark night within his traitorous breast.

Now, brethren, the same Savior is this day in the midst of us. He walks in the midst of the seven gold candlesticks—His eyes are like a flame of fire, and He searches the reins and the hearts. *Think of this, you that are open sinners*, and yet dare to sit down at the table of Christ—swearers—drunkards—Sabbath breakers—unclean. Ministers and elders may not know your sins; they are weak and short-sighted men. Your very neighbors may not know your sins; you may hide them from your own family. It is easy to deceive man; but to deceive Christ is impossible. He knows your whole history; He is present at every act of dishonesty—of filthiness—of folly. The darkness and the light are both alike to Him. *Think of this, you that live in heart-sins*, rolling sin beneath your tongue as a sweet morsel—you that put on the outward cloak of seriousness and sobriety that you may jostle and sit down among the children of God—you that have the speech of Canaan in your lips, but hatred and malice, and the very breath of hell in your hearts—you that have the clothing of sheep, but inwardly are ravening wolves—you that are whited sepulchers, beautiful without, but within full of dead men's bones and all uncleanness. Think of this, you that know yourselves unconverted, and yet have dared to sit down at the table of Christ. Christ knows you—Christ could point to you—Christ could name you—Christ could give the sop to you. You may be hidden to all the world, but you are naked and open to the eyes of Him with whom you have to do. Oh! that you would fall down beneath His piercing glance, and say: "God be merciful to me, a sinner!" Oh! that every one of you would say: "Lord, is it I?"

Christ's Love Used to Win Judas' Heart

The second argument which Christ made use of to melt

and win the heart of Judas was His love: I have loved you, Judas, and came to save you.

1. This was plainly His intention when washing the disciples' feet. He did not shrink from the traitor's feet; yes, He not only stooped to wash the feet of those who were to forsake Him and flee—He not only washed the feet of Peter, who was, before the cock crowed, to deny Him with oaths and curses—but He washed also the feet of Judas, the very feet which had gone, two days before, to the meeting of priests in Caiaphas' palace where he sold the Savior for thirty pieces of silver, the value of a slave; and it was in his hearing He spoke the gentle words: "If I wash thee not, thou hast no part with me." If, then, the Savior's washing the feet of the eleven was so blessed a proof of His tenderness to His own disciples, how much more is His washing the feet of him who (He knew) had betrayed Him, a proof of His love to sinners, even the chief! He willed not the death of Judas—He wills not the death of any one of you. You think that because you have betrayed the Savior and come to the feast without any warrant or title, an unbidden intruder, therefore Jesus cannot love you. Alas! this shows your own heart, but not Christ's heart. Behold Jesus washing the feet of Judas and wiping them with the towel wherewith He was girded; behold His anxiety to awaken and to win the heart of the traitor Judas. And then think how the more you are a traitor and a betrayer, the more Jesus pities you and waits upon you, willing still to wash and to save you saying: "Turn ye, turn ye, why will ye die?"

2. The *second* instance of Jesus' love to the traitor is when He had sat down again and was eating the Passover along with the other eleven, He did not shrink from eating meat with the traitor. Yes, He not only sat down to eat with the eleven who were to forsake Him and flee— He not only allowed John to recline on His bosom and Peter to sit at the table, but He suffered Judas to dip his hand in the very same dish with Him, even when He knew that he was fulfilling that prophecy which is written, "He that eateth bread with me, hath lifted up his heel against me." It was a blessed proof of the Savior's

love to His believing disciples, as is recorded by Luke when he said: "With desire have I desired to eat this Passover with you before I suffer." One would have thought that to the eye of the Savior this Passover must have appeared covered with threatening clouds—involved in the deep gloom of the garden of Gethsemane, and the bloody cross from which the sun himself hid his beams. You always find that when you are in immediate expectation of some calamity; it renders gloomy and uninviting every event that bespeaks its near approach.

You would have thought, then, that the human soul of Jesus must have shrunk back from this Passover with horror. But no, he felt the shrinking of humanity which more plainly showed itself in the garden. But His love for His own disciples was stronger than all beside, and made Him look forward to this Passover when He was to picture out to them His dying love more clearly than ever with intense desire: "With desire have I desired to eat this passover with you before I suffer." But how much more wonderful is the proof of the Savior's love to the unbelieving—to those who care not for Him, but are His betrayers and murderers—when, with such divine complacency, He dips His hand in the same dish with Judas and tells him, at the same time, that He does it not through ignorance, but that the prophecy might be fulfilled: "He that eateth bread with me, hath lifted up the heel against me."

Ah! my unbelieving friends, I know well the dark suspicions that lurk in your bosoms. Because you have done everything against Christ, you think that He cannot have any love for you; but behold, dark and proud sinners, how lovingly, how tenderly, He tries, if it may be, to awaken and to win over the heart of Judas! And then think how anxious He is this day to win and awaken you, though you are of sinners the chief—to bow that brazen neck—to break that heart of adamant—to wring a tear from those eyes that never wept for sin.

3. The *third* instance of Jesus' love to the traitor is His faithful declaration of his danger to him: "The Son of Man goeth, as it is written of him; but woe unto that

man by whom the Son of Man is betrayed! It had been good for that man if he had never been born." In the two former instances Jesus had shown His love by showing how willing He was to save him to the very uttermost—that He would bear all things to save him; but now He uses another way—He shows him the terror of the Lord—tells him that if he will persist, "it had been good for him that he had not been born."

As a mother, when she wishes her child to take some wholesome medicine, first wins upon its love, and then, if that will not do, tries to win upon its fears; with the same, more than mother's tenderness, did Jesus first try to win upon the affections, and now upon the fears of Judas. And He is the same Savior this day in the upper chambers of the universe that He was that night in the upper chamber at Jerusalem; and He sends His messengers to you to carry the same messages of kindness and of love. It is only in love that He threatens you. And, oh! that in love we might speak the threatening to you—that if you have no part in Jesus, and yet, by sitting down at His table, are becoming guilty of the body and blood of our Lord, it were better for you that you had not been born.

It is a happy thing to live; there is a blessedness which cannot be expressed in having life. The fly that lives but for a day—the veriest worm or insect that crawls upon the ground has an amount of blessedness in the very fact that it lives, which it is far beyond the skill of man to calculate. To breathe, to move, to feel the morning sun and the evening breeze—to look out upon the green world and the blue sky—all this is happiness immense—immeasurable.

It never can be said of a fly or worm that it had better never been born; but, alas! it may be said of some of you: If you are living, but not living united to Christ—if you are sitting at the table of Christ, and yet unconverted—it had been good for you that you had not been born.

Ah! my friends, there was once a heathen man who always wept, and got the name of the Weeping Philosopher. One would almost think that he had known this

truth which we preach unto you—that if that union which
you make with the bread and wine at the holy table be
not a picture and a seal of the union between your soul
and the Savior of sinners, you had far better never have
been born. Better not to be, than to be only in hell.
"They shall wish to die, and shall not be able; they shall
seek to die, and death shall flee from them."

4. The *fourth* and last instance of Jesus' love to the
traitor is the most touching of all. After the Supper was
over, *Jesus was troubled in spirit*, and testified and said:
"Verily, verily, I say unto you, that one of you shall
betray me."

It was but a few days before that He came riding
down the declivity of Mount Olivet upon an ass' colt; and
His disciples, behind and before, were all rejoicing and
praising God, crying "Hosanna!" and Jesus—what was
He doing? He was weeping: "When he came near, he
beheld the city, and wept over it, saying, If thou hadst
known, even thou, at least in this thy day, the things
that belong unto thy peace! but now they are hid from
thine eyes." He wept over the very city which He doomed
to destruction.

And just so here: when His disciples on every hand
were filled with a holy joy, and John most of all rejoicing, for he lay in the bosom of Immanuel, what was
Christ doing—the author of all their joy? He was heavy
and troubled in spirit. He was always the man of sorrows, and acquainted with grief, but now a ruffle of deeper
sorrow came over the placid calm of His holy features—
He was troubled in spirit, and said: "Verily, verily, I say
unto you, one of you shall betray me." He had tried all
arguments to move His betrayer—He had unbosomed
the tenderness of His love—He had shown the dreadful-
ness of His anger. But when He saw that all would not
do to move his hard heart—when He saw the heartless
unconcern with which Judas could swallow down the
bread, and share in the blessed cup, the spirit of the
Savior sank within Him; and the last effort of His love to
awaken the impenitent murderer was, to unbosom the
depth of His sorrows and to breathe out with many sighs

the words: "Verily, verily, I say unto you, that one of you shall betray me."

My friends, there may be some within these walls with a heart as hard as that of Judas. Like Judas, you are about to partake of the most moving ordinance the world ever saw; like Judas, you may eat of the bread and drink of the wine; and like Judas, your heart may grow harder, and your life more sinful than ever. And you think, then, that Jesus is your enemy? But what does the Bible say? Look here: He is troubled in spirit—He weeps as He did over Jerusalem. Yes, He that once shed His blood for you, now sheds His tears for you. Immanuel grieves that you will not be saved. He grieved over Judas, and He grieves over you. He wept over Jerusalem, and He weeps over you. He has no pleasure that you should perish—He had far rather that you would turn and have life.

There is not within these walls one of you so hard, so cruel, so base, so unmoved, so far from grace and godliness, so Judas-like that Jesus does not grieve over your hardness—that you will still resist all His love—that you will still love death, and wrong your own soul. Oh! that the tears which the Savior shed over your lost and perishing souls might fall upon your hearts like drops of liquid fire—that you might no more sit unmelted under that wondrous love which burns with so vehement a flame—which many waters cannot quench—which all your sin cannot smother—the love which passes knowledge. Amen.

The Last Pleading of Love

Alexander Maclaren (1826–1910) was one of Great Britain's most famous preachers. While pastoring the Union Chapel, Manchester (1858–1903), he became known as "the prince of expository preachers." Rarely active in denominational or civic affairs, Maclaren invested his time in studying the Word in the original and sharing its truths with others in sermons that are still models of effective expository preaching. He published a number of books of sermons and climaxed his ministry by publishing his monumental *Expositions of Holy Scripture*. This message is taken from that series, the volume covering Matthew 18–28.

Alexander Maclaren

11

THE LAST PLEADING OF LOVE

And Jesus said unto him, Friend, wherefore art thou come?
(Matthew 26:50).

WE ARE ACCUSTOMED to think of the betrayer of our Lord
as a kind of monster, whose crime is so mysterious in its
atrocity as to put him beyond the pale of human sympathy.
The awful picture which the great Italian poet draws of
him as alone in hell, shunned even there, as guilty beyond
all others, expresses the general feeling about him. And
even the attempts which have been made to diminish the
greatness of his guilt, by supposing that his motive was
only to precipitate Christ's assumption of His conquering
Messianic power, are prompted by the same thought that
such treason as his is all but inconceivable. I cannot but
think that these attempts fail, and that the narratives of
the Gospels oblige us to think of his crime as deliberate
treachery. But even when so regarded, other emotions
than wondering loathing should be excited by the awful
story.

There had been nothing in his previous history to suggest such sin, as is proved by the disciples' question, when
our Lord announced that one of them should betray Him.
No suspicion lighted on him—no finger pointed to where
he sat. But self-distrust asked, "Lord, is it I?" and only
love, pillowed on the Master's breast, and strong in the
happy sense of His love, was sufficiently assured of its
own constancy, to change the question into "Lord! who is
it?" The process of corruption was unseen by all eyes but
Christ's. He came to his terrible preeminence in crime by
slow degrees, and by paths which we may all tread. As for
his guilt, that is in other hands than ours. As for his fate,
let us copy the solemn and pitying reticence of Peter, and
say, "that he might go to his own place"—the place that

belongs to him, and that he is fit for, wherever that may be. As for the growth and development of his sin, let us remember that "we have all of us one human heart," and that the possibilities of crime as dark are in us all. And instead of shuddering abhorrence at a sin that can scarcely be understood, and can never be repeated, let us be sure that whatever man has done, man may do, and ask with humble consciousness of our own deceitful hearts, "Lord, is it I?"

These remarkable and solemn words of Christ, with which He meets the treacherous kiss, appear to be a last appeal to Judas. They may possibly not be a question, as in our version—but an incomplete sentence, "What thou hast come to do"—leaving the implied command, "That do," unexpressed. They would then be very like other words which the betrayer had heard but an hour or two before, "That thou doest, do quickly." But such a rendering does not seem so appropriate to the circumstances as that which makes them a question, smiting on his heart and conscience, and seeking to tear away the veil of sophistications with which he had draped from his own eyes the hideous shape of his crime. And, if so, what a wonderful instance we have here of that long-suffering love. They are the last effort of the divine patience to win back even the traitor. They show us the wrestle between infinite mercy and a treacherous, sinful heart, and they bring into awful prominence the power which that heart has of rejecting the counsel of God against itself. I venture to use them now as suggesting these three things: the patience of Christ's love, the pleading of Christ's love, and the refusal of Christ's love.

The Patience of Christ's Love

If we take no higher view of this most pathetic incident than that the words come from a man's lips, even then all its beauty will not be lost. There are some sins against friendship in which the manner is harder to bear than the substance of the evil. It must have been a strangely mean and dastardly nature, as well as a coarse and cold one, that could think of fixing on the kiss of affection as the concerted sign to point out their victim to the legionaries. Many a man who could have planned and executed the treason would have shrunk from that. And many a man who could have born to be betrayed by his own familiar friend would have found that heartless insult worse to endure than the treason itself.

But what a picture of perfect patience and unruffled calm we have here in that the answer to the poisonous, hypocritical embrace was these moving words! The touch of the traitor's lips has barely left His cheek, but not one faint passing flush of anger tinges it. He is perfectly self-oblivious—absorbed in other thought, and among them in pity for the guilty wretch before Him. His words have no agitation in them, no instinctive recoil from the pollution of such a salutation. They have grave rebuke, but it is rebuke which derives its very force from the appeal to former companionship. Christ still recognizes the ancient bond, and is true to it. He will still plead with this man who has been beside Him long; and though His heart be wounded yet He is not wroth, and He will not cast him off. If this were nothing more than a picture of human friendship it would stand alone, above all other records that the world cherishes in its inmost heart, of the love that never fails, and is not soon angry.

But we, I hope, dear brethren, think more loftily and more truly of our dear Lord than as simply a perfect manhood, the exemplar of all goodness. How He comes to be that, if He be not more than that, I do not understand, and I, for one, feel that my confidence in the flawless completeness of His human character lives or dies with my belief that He is the Eternal Word, God manifest in the flesh. Certainly we shall never truly grasp the blessed meaning of His life on earth until we look upon it all as the revelation of God. The tears of Christ are the pity of God. The gentleness of Jesus is the long-suffering of God. The tenderness of Jesus is the love of God. "He that hath seen Me hath seen the Father"; and all that life so beautiful but so anomalous as to be all but incredible, when we think of it as only the life of a man, glows with a yet fairer beauty, and corresponds with the nature which it expresses, when we think of it as being the declaration to us by the divine Son of the divine Father—our loftiest, clearest, and authentic revelation of God.

How that thought lifts these words before us into a still higher region! We are now in the presence of the solemn greatness of a divine love. If the meaning of this saying is what we have suggested, it is pathetic even in the lower aspect, but how infinitely that pathos is deepened when we view it in the higher!

Surely if ever there was a man who might have been supposed to be excluded from the love of God, it was Judas. Surely if ever there was a moment in a human life when one might have supposed that even Christ's ever open heart would shut itself together against anyone, it was this moment. But no, the betrayer in the very instant of his treason has that changeless tenderness lingering around him and that merciful hand beckoning to him still.

And have we not a right to generalize this wonderful fact, and to declare its teaching to be—that the love of God is extended to us all, and cannot be made to turn away from us by any sins of ours? Sin is mighty; it can work endless evils on us; it can disturb and embitter all our relations with God; it can, as we shall presently have to point out, make it necessary for the tenderest "grace of God to come disciplining"—to "come with a rod," just because it comes in "the spirit of meekness." But one thing it cannot do, and that is—make God cease to love us.

I suppose all human affection can be worn out by constant failure to evoke a response from cold hearts. I suppose that it can be so nipped by frosts, so constantly checked in blossoming, that it shrivels and dies. I suppose that constant ingratitude, constant indifference can turn the warmest springs of our love to a river of ice. "Can a mother forget her child?—Yes, she may forget." But we have to do with a God, whose love is His very being, who loves us not for reasons in us but in Himself, whose love is eternal and boundless as all His nature, whose love, therefore, cannot be turned away by our sin—but abides with us forever and is granted to every soul of man. Dear brethren, we cannot believe too firmly, we cannot trust too absolutely, we cannot proclaim too broadly that blessed thought, without which we have no hope to feed on for ourselves or to share with our fellows—the universal love of God in Christ.

Is there a *worst* man on earth at this moment? If there be, he too has a share in that love. Harlots and thieves, publicans and sinners, leprous outcasts, and souls tormented by unclean spirits, the wrecks of humanity whom decent society and respectable Christianity passes by with averted head and uplifted hands, criminals on the gibbet with the rope around their necks—and those who are as hopeless as any of these, self-complacent formalists and "gospel-hardened professors"—all have a place in that heart. And that, not as undistinguished members of a class, but as separate souls, singly the objects of God's knowledge and love.

He loves all, because He loves each. We are not massed together in His view, nor in His regard. He does not lose the details in the whole, as we, looking on some great crowd of upturned faces, are conscious of all but recognize no single one. He does not love a class—a world—but He loves the single souls that make it up—you and me, and every one of the millions that we throw together in the vague phrase, "the race." Let us individualize that love in our thoughts as it individualizes us in its outflow—and make our own the "exceeding broad" promises, which include us too. "God loves *me*; Christ gave Himself for *me*. I have a place in that royal, tender heart."

Nor should any sin make us doubt this, He loved us with exceeding love, even when we were "dead in trespasses." He did not begin to love because of anything in us; He will not cease because of anything in us. We change; "He abideth faithful, He cannot deny Himself." As the sunshine pours down as willingly and abundantly on filth and dunghills, as on gold that glitters in its beam, and jewels that flash back its luster, so the light and warmth of that unsetting and unexhausted source of life pours down "on the unthankful and on the good." The great ocean clasps some black and barren crag that frowns against it, as closely as with its waves it kisses some fair strand enameled with flowers and fragrant with perfumes. So that sea of love in which we "live, and move, and have our being," encircles the worst with abundant flow. He Himself sets us the pattern, which to imitate is to be the children of "our Father which is in heaven," in that He loves His enemies, blessing them that curse, and doing good to them that hate. He Himself is what He has enjoined us to be in that He feeds His enemies when they hunger, and when they thirst gives them drink, heaping coals of fire on their heads, and seeking to kindle in them thereby the glow of answering love, not being overcome of their evil, so that He repays hate with hate and scorn with scorn, but in patient continuance of loving kindness seeking to overcome evil with good. He is Himself that "charity" which "is not easily provoked, is not soon angry, bears all things, hopes all things, and never fails." His love is mightier than all our sins, and waits not on our merits, nor is turned away by our iniquities. "God so loved the world that He gave His only-begotten Son, that whosoever believeth in Him should not perish, but have everlasting life."

The Pleading of Christ's Love

I have been trying to say as broadly and strongly as I can, that our sins do not turn away the love of God in Christ from us. The more earnestly we believe and proclaim that, the more needful is it to set forth distinctly— and that not as limiting, but as explaining the truth—the other thought that the sin which does not avert does modify the expression of the love of God. Man's sin compels Him to do what the prophet calls his "strange work"—the work which is not dear to His heart, nor natural, if one may so say, to His hands—His work of judgment.

The love of Christ has to come to sinful men with patient pleading and remonstrance that it may enter their hearts and give its blessings. We are familiar with a modern work of art in which that long-suffering appeal is wonderfully portrayed. He who is the Light of the world stands, girded with the royal mantle clasped with the priestly breastplate, bearing in His hand the lamp of truth, and there, amidst the dew of night and the rank hemlock, He pleads for entrance at the closed door which has no handle on its outer side and is hinged to open only from within. "I stand at the door and knock. If any man open the door, I will come in."

And in this incident before us, we see represented not only the endless patience of God's pitying love, but the method which it needs to take in order to reach the heart.

There is an appeal to the traitor's heart, and an appeal to his conscience. Christ would have him think of the relations that have so long subsisted between them; and He would have him think, too, of the real nature of the deed he is doing, or, perhaps, of the motives that impel him. The grave, sad word, by which He addresses him, is meant to smite upon his heart. The sharp question which He puts to him is meant to wake up his conscience; and both taken together represent the two chief classes of remonstrance which He brings to bear upon us all—the two great batteries from which He assails the fortress of our sins.

There is first, then—Christ's appeal to the heart. He tries to make Judas feel the considerations that should restrain him. The appellation by which our Lord addresses him does not in the original convey quite so strongly the idea of amity as our word "Friend" does. It is not the same as that which He had used a few hours before in the upper chamber when He said, "Henceforth I call you not servants, but I have called you friends. Ye are My friends if ye do whatsoever I command you." It is the same as is put into the lips of the Lord of the vineyard, remonstrating with his jealous laborer, "Friend, I do thee no wrong."

There is a tone, then, of less intimate association and graver rebuke in it than in that name with which He honors those who make His will theirs, and His word the law of their lives. It does not speak of close confidence, but it does suggest companionship and kindness on the part of the speaker. There is rebuke in it, but it is rebuke which derives its whole force from the remembrance of ancient concord and connection. Our Lord would recall to the memory of the betrayer the days in which they had taken sweet counsel together. It is as if He had said—"Have you forgotten all our former friendship? You have eaten My bread, you have been Mine own familiar friend, in whom I trusted—can you lift up your heel against Me?"

What happy hours of quiet fellowship on many a journey, of rest together after many a day of toil, what forgotten thoughts of the loving devotion and the glow of glad consecration that he had once felt, what a long series of proofs of Christ's gentle goodness and meek wisdom should have sprung again to remembrance at such an appeal! And how black and dastardly would his guilt have seemed if once he had ventured to remember what unexampled friendship he was sinning against!

Is it not so with us all, dear brethren? All our evils are betrayals of Christ, and all our betrayals of Christ are sins against a perfect friendship and an unvaried goodness. We too have sat at His table, heard His wisdom, seen His miracles, listened to His pleadings, have had a place in His heart; and if we turn away from Him to do our own pleasure, and sell His love for a handful of silver, we need not cherish shuddering abhorrence against that poor wretch who gave Him up to the cross. Oh! if we could see aright, we should see our Savior's meek, sad face standing between us and each of our sins, with warning in the pitying eyes, and His pleading voice would sound in our ears, appealing to us by loving remembrances of His ancient friendship, to turn from the evil which is treason against Him and wounds His heart as much as it harms ours. Take heed lest in condemning the traitor we doom ourselves. If we flush into anger at the meanness of his crime, and declare, "He shall surely die," do we not hear a prophet's voice saying to each, "Thou art the man"?

The loving hand laid on the heartstrings is followed by a strong stroke on conscience. The heart vibrates most readily in answer to gentle touches: the conscience, in answer to heavier, as the breath that wakes the chords of an Æolian harp would pass silent through the brass of a trumpet. "Wherefore art thou come?"—if to be taken as a question at all, which, as I have said, seems most natural, is either, "What hast thou come to do?"—or, "Why hast thou come to do it?" Perhaps it may be fairly taken as including both. But at all events, it is clearly an appeal to Judas to make him see what his conduct really is in itself, and possibly in its motive too. And this is the constant effort of the love of Christ—to get us to say to ourselves the real name of what we are about.

We cloak our sins from ourselves with many wrappings, as they swathe a mummy in voluminous folds. And of these veils, one of the thickest is woven by our misuse of words to describe the very same thing by different names, according as we do it, or another man does it. Almost all moral actions—the thing to which we can apply the words right or wrong—have two or more names, of which the one suggests the better and the other the worse side of the action.

For instance what in ourselves we call prudent regard for our own interest, we call in our neighbor narrow selfishness; what in ourselves is laudable economy, in him is miserable avarice. We are impetuous, he is passionate; we generous, he lavish; we are clever men of business, he is a rogue; we sow our wild oats and are happy, he is dissipated. So we cheat ourselves by more than half-transparent veils of our own manufacture, which we fling around the ugly features and misshapen limbs of these sins of ours, and we are made more than ever their bondslaves thereby.

Therefore, it is the office of the truest love to force us to look at the thing as it is. It would go some way to keep a man from some of his sins if he would give the thing its real name. A distinct conscious statement to oneself, "Now I am going to tell a lie"—"This that I am doing is fraud"—"This emotion that I feel creeping with devilish warmth about the roots of my heart is revenge"—and so on, would surely startle us sometimes, and make us fling the gliding poison from our breast, as a man would a snake that he found just lifting its head from the bosom of his robe.

Suppose Judas had answered the question, and, gathering himself up, had looked his Master in the face, and

said—"What have I come for?" "I have come to betray
Thee for thirty pieces of silver!" Do you not think that
putting his guilt into words might have moved even him
to more salutary feelings than the remorse which afterward accompanied his tardy discernment of what he *had*
done? So the patient love of Christ comes rebuking, and
smiting hard on conscience. "The grace of God that bringeth
salvation to all men hath appeared disciplining"—and His
hand is never more gentle than when it plucks away the
films with which we hide our sins from ourselves, and
shows us the "rottenness and dead men's bones" beneath
the whited walls of the sepulchers and the velvet of the
coffins.

He must begin with rebukes that He may advance to
blessing. He must teach us what is separating us from
Him that, learning it, we may flee to His grace to help us.
There is no entrance for the truest gifts of His patient
love into any heart that has not yielded to His pleading
remonstrance, and in lowly penitence has answered His
question as He would have us answer it, "Friend and
Lover of my soul, I have sinned against Your tender heart,
against the unexampled patience of Your love. I have
departed from You and betrayed You. Blessed be Your
merciful voice which has taught me what I have done!
Blessed be Your unwearied goodness which still bends
over me! Raise me fallen! Forgive me treacherous! Keep
me safe and happy, ever true and near to You!"

The Refusal of Christ's Love

Even that appeal was vain. Here we are confronted
with a plain instance of man's mysterious and awful
power of "frustrating the counsel of God"—of which one
knows not whether is greater, the difficulty of understanding how a finite will *can* rear itself against the
Infinite Will, or the mournful mystery that a creature
should desire to set itself against its loving Maker and
Benefactor. But strange as it is, yet so it is; and we can
turn around upon Sovereign Fatherhood bidding us to
its service, and say, "*I will not.*" He pleads with us, and
we can resist His pleadings. He holds out the mercies of

His hands and the gifts of His grace, and we can reject them. We cannot cease to be the objects of His love, but we can refuse to be the recipients of its most precious gifts. We can bar our hearts against it. Then, of what avail is it to us? To go back to an earlier illustration, the sunshine pours down and floods a world, what does that matter to us if we have fastened up shutters on all our windows, and barred every crevice through which the streaming gladness can find its way? We shall grope at noontide as in the dark within our gloomy house, while our neighbors have light in theirs. What matters it though we float in the great ocean of the divine love, if with pitch and canvas we have carefully closed every aperture at which the flood can enter? A hermetically closed jar, plunged in the Atlantic, will be as dry inside as if it were lying on the sand of the desert. It is possible to perish of thirst within sight of the fountain. It is possible to separate ourselves from the love of God, not to separate the love of God from ourselves.

The incident before us carries another solemn lesson—how simple and easy a thing it is to repel that pleading love. What did Judas do? Nothing; it was enough. He merely held his peace—no more. There was no need for him to break out with oaths and curses, to reject his Lord with wild words. Silence was sufficient. And for us—no more is required. We have but to be passive; we have but to stand still. Not to accept is to refuse; nonsubmission is rebellion. We do not need to emphasize our refusal by any action—no need to lift our clenched hands in defiance. We have simply to put them behind our backs or to keep them folded. The closed hand must remain an empty hand. "He that believeth not is condemned." My friend, remember that, when Christ pleads and draws, to do nothing is to oppose, and to delay is to refuse. It is a very easy matter to ruin your soul. You have simply to keep still when He says, "Come unto Me"—to keep your eyes fixed where they were when He says, "Look unto Me, and be ye saved," and all the rest will follow of itself.

Notice too how the appeal of Christ's love hardens where it does not soften. That gentle voice drove the traitor nearer the verge over which he fell into a gulf of despair. It should have drawn him closer to the Lord, but he recoiled from it, and was thereby brought nearer destruction. Every pleading of Christ's grace, whether by providences, or by books, or by His own word, does something with us. It is never vain. Either it melts or it hardens. The sun either scatters the summer morning mists, or it rolls them into heavier folds, from whose livid depths the lightning will be flashing by mid-day. You cannot come near the most inadequate exhibition of the pardoning love of Christ without being either drawn closer to Him or driven further from Him. Each act of rejection prepares the way for another, which will be easier, and adds another film to the darkness which covers your eyes, another layer to the hardness which encrusts your hearts.

Again, that silence, so eloquent and potent in its influence, was probably the silence of a man whose conscience was convicted while his will was unchanged. Such a condition is possible. It points to solemn thoughts, and to deep mysteries in man's awful nature. He knew that he was wrong, he had no excuse, his deed was before him in some measure in its true character, and yet he would not give it up. Such a state, if constant and complete, presents the most frightful picture we can frame of a soul. That a man shall not be able to say, "I did it ignorantly," that Christ shall not be able to ground His intercession on, "They know not what they do," that with full knowledge of the true nature of the deed, there shall be no wavering of the determination to do it—we may well turn with terror from such an awful abyss. But let us remember that, whether such a condition in its completeness is conceivable or not, at all events we may approach it indefinitely; and we do approach it by every sin, and by every refusal to yield to the love that would touch our consciences and fill our hearts.

Have you ever noticed what a remarkable verbal correspondence there is between these words of our text and some other very solemn ones of Christ's? The question that He puts into the lips of the king who came in to see his guests is, *"Friend, how camest thou* in hither, not having on a wedding garment?" The question asked on earth shall be repeated again at last. The silence which once indicated a convinced conscience and an unchanged will may at that day indicate both of these and hopelessness beside. The clear vision of the divine love, if it do not flood the heart with joy and evoke the bliss of answering love, may fill it with bitterness. It is possible that the same revelation of the same grace may be the heaven of heaven to those who welcome it, and the pain of hell to those who turn from it. It is possible that love believed and received may be life, and love recognized and rejected may be death. It is possible that the vision of the same face may make some break forth with the rapturous hymn, "Lo, this is our God, we have waited for Him!" and make others call on the hills to fall on them and cover them from its brightness.

But let us not end with such words. Rather, dear brethren, let us yield to His patient beseechings; let Him teach us our evil and our sin. Listen to His great love who invites us to plead, and promises to pardon—"Come now, and let us reason together, saith the Lord: though your sins be as scarlet, they shall be as white as snow; though they be red like crimson, they shall be as wool."